OXFORD
UNIVERSITY PRESS

Oxford University Press, Inc., publishes works that further
Oxford University's objective of excellence
in research, scholarship, and education.

Oxford   New York
Auckland   Cape Town   Dar es Salaam   Hong Kong   Karachi
Kuala Lumpur   Madrid   Melbourne   Mexico City   Nairobi
New Delhi   Shanghai   Taipei   Toronto

With offices in
Argentina   Austria   Brazil   Chile   Czech Republic   France   Greece
Guatemala   Hungary   Italy   Japan   Poland   Portugal   Singapore
South Korea   Switzerland   Thailand   Turkey   Ukraine   Vietnam

Published by Oxford University Press, Inc.
198 Madison Avenue, New York, NY 10016

www.oup.com

Oxford is a registered trademark of Oxford University Press

Library of Congress Cataloging-in-Publication Data
Metcalf, Allan A.
OK : the improbable story of America's greatest word /
Allan Metcalf.
p.   cm.
Includes index.
ISBN 978-0-19-537793-4
1. English language—United States—Etymology.
2. United States—History—Terminology.
3. English language—Usage. 4. Americanisms. I. Title.
PE2831.M48 2010
427′.973—dc21
2010009709

1 3 5 7 9 8 6 4 2

Printed in the United States of America
on acid-free paper

OK

THE IMPROBABLE STORY OF
AMERICA'S GREATEST WORD

Allan Metcalf

UNIVERSITY PRESS

2011

To the memory of
Allen Walker Read
who rules OK

CONTENTS

PREFACE

··················

OK. WHY THIS BOOK? STRANGELY ENOUGH, EVEN THOUGH
OK is by far the most successful American creation in language, as
well as nearly the strangest, it hasn't had a book of its own. So here
it is.

And it is made possible, above all, by Allen Walker Read
(1906–2002), professor at Columbia University, scholar without
equal of American English. Before he came along, a century of
speculation, obfuscation, and deliberate deception had obscured
the origin of OK seemingly beyond recovery. In the absence of any
clear evidence and the presence of false rumors, learned lexicogra-
phers as well as ordinary citizens were free to imagine the beginnings of OK in sources as disparate as the Choctaw Indian
language, Otto Kimmel's biscuits, and supposed misspelling by

President Andrew Jackson. All plausible, in their way, but as Read would demonstrate, O.R. (all wrong).

His name was apt, because Read read voluminously in the books, magazines, and newspapers of early America. He did this as a staff member of the four-volume scholarly *Dictionary of American English* (1938–44) but also on his own throughout his life. So it was not surprising that Read was the one who discovered, in fine print on page 2 of the *Boston Morning Post* of March 23, 1839, an instance of OK that turned out to be the earliest on record. Nobody else but Read would have been combing through that newspaper looking for words, and nobody else but Read had read widely enough in the newspapers of that day to be sure that this was the first instance.

When he published his findings in a series of articles in the journal *American Speech* back in 1963–64, he didn't offer just that one citation. To prove his point beyond dispute, he provided literally hundreds of quotations from newspapers of the 1830s and 1840s, showing not only the context of joking abbreviations and misspelling that made OK possible in the first place but also the growth and development of OK as it was adapted in the presidential election of 1840 for "Old Kinderhook," Martin Van Buren, and for many subsequent purposes.

Since the publication of his articles, there have been occasional challenges to Read's evidence of the origin of OK in that Boston newspaper. All have failed to earn support, however, because they rest either entirely on speculation or on isolated instances of something written earlier. As for speculation, it's easy to find native expressions in other languages that sound like OK—that's one reason why the American OK has spread so widely through the languages of the world. But speculation needs evidence to back it, and so far none has been found. As for the earlier isolated instances, some have turned out to be misreadings, while others—well, there's not a shred of evidence showing that one night's watchword from the American Revolution was somehow connected with a Boston joke half a century later.

My chapters on the first few years of OK necessarily lean heavily on Read's evidence. Those who have seen his articles in *American Speech* or their reprint in his *Milestones in the History of English in America* (edited by Richard W. Bailey, Publication of the American Dialect Society 86, Duke University Press, 2002) will recognize much that is familiar here. The additional matter in my chapters only further confirms his conclusions.

In the half century since Read's articles, much more has been discovered about the later life of OK as it developed from joke to business tool and then to staple of everyday conversation and an attitude toward life. A wealth of new material is available, unimaginable in the paper world of fifty years ago. Internet, take a bow.

I have tried to be as generous as Read in providing examples to illustrate the development of OK. The vast majority of examples come from the Internet, many of them in historical document databases such as Making of America, a digital collection of nineteenth-century newspapers, magazines, and books. Mining the data for examples of OK is still hard work; there is much fool's gold in the false positives dredged up from old publications by automatic OCR. Nevertheless, searching the Internet for OK locates many needles in acres of haystacks, allowing for a full-length portrait that begins to do justice to this incomparable expression.

You won't find footnotes in this book. The Internet changes too fast for that. Instead, I have tried to acknowledge sources in sufficient detail that you can locate them too by Googling, with a little luck. In those places in my book I have named the numerous people who, wittingly or un-, have contributed to this portrait of OK.

But in addition, let me here note my gratitude for help in ways beyond those noted in the text from researchers Erin McKean, Richard W. Bailey, Barry Popik, Joseph Pickett, and James Davis; at MacMurray College from Colleen Hester, Alice Dodson, Malea Harney, Linda Duncan, Nadine Szczepanski, Dan Currier, Susan Eilering, and DeeAnn Roome; and elsewhere from Fr. Kip Ashmore, Sara Metcalf, Ginger Lane, Elizabeth Schneewind, Jennifer Choi, and Louise DeCosta Wides. At Oxford University Press I had essential assistance from Peter Ohlin, Brian Hurley, Lucy Randall, Woody Gilmartin, Joellyn Ausanka, and Betsy DeJesu. And I must reserve my last word of thanks for my wife, Donna, who is way beyond OK.

OK? Let's begin.

INTRODUCTION
THE ABCS OF OK

IT IS SAID TO BE THE MOST FREQUENTLY SPOKEN (OR TYPED) word on the planet, bigger even than an infant's first word *ma* or the ubiquitous *Coke*. And it was the first word spoken on the moon.

It's America's answer to Shakespeare.

It's an entire philosophy expressed in two letters.

It's very odd, but it's . . . OK.

Yes, OK. Just two simple letters. And two letters of humble origin; they were born as a lame joke perpetrated by a newspaper editor in 1839. But these two simple letters (or four, if you use its genteel alter ego *okay*) anchor our agreements, confirm our understandings, and choreograph the dance of everyday life.

This is a book about OK. And OK truly deserves a book of its own, not only because it is different from anything else in our language but because it is so important. OK is a meme that has burrowed deeply into the way we think and act. In fact, those two letters encapsulate a whole view of life—the American philosophy, if two letters can be said to embody a philosophy, and if Americans can be said to have one.

Yet we scarcely notice. OK seems too simple, too trivial, and above all too familiar to attract notice to itself. It scarcely makes an appearance in books of famous quotations. Here, in fact, is the complete *Book of Famous OK Quotations:*

I'm OK—You're OK

—*Title of book on transactional analysis (1967) by Thomas A. Harris, M.D.*

That's it? Yes, to capture all the famous quotations involving *love* or *war* would take many pages. But the collection of famous quotations involving OK contains all of one item.

Wait a minute, you might say. What about Todd Beamer's famous "OK, let's roll!" to begin the attack on the terrorists who hijacked United Flight 93 on September 11, 2001? The full quotation was "Are you guys ready? OK, let's roll!" But even in that statement, the OK was inconspicuous. On the T-shirts and other memorabilia that soon were produced in his honor, only the last two words were reproduced. His wife Lisa's book honoring him likewise omitted OK from its title: *Let's Roll! Ordinary People, Extraordinary Courage.* As *Time* magazine summarized in December 2001, "Many diverse Americans have latched onto his phrase 'Let's roll' to symbolize that strength of character." But not OK.

It's everywhere, but hardly noticed. In the November 23, 2009, issue of the *New Yorker* you will find a cartoon whose caption begins and ends with OK. Two waiters are standing in an entrance-way looking at a woman at a distant table, and one says to the other, "O.K., her mouth is full—run over and ask her if everything is O.K." Amusing, but not because of OK. And there's no indication that the joke was making any kind of play on the two different meanings of OK that it employs.

No Bananas

Another missed opportunity for a famous OK quotation came when Frank Silver and Irving Cohn wrote one of the best-known songs of the twentieth century. In an alternate universe, maybe, their lyrics would go like this:

> There's a fruit store on our street.
> It's run by a Greek.
> And he keeps good things to eat,
> But you should hear him speak.
> When you ask him anything,
> Never answers no.
> He just OKs you to death,
> And as he take your dough, he tells you:
> "OK! We have no bananas. We have no bananas today. . . ."

But in our universe, because of the unassuming nature of OK, Silver and Cohn instead chose a different word for their 1923 hit, and the quotation books have only "Yes! We have no bananas."

Important, yet inconspicuous. That is just one of the oddities of the world's best-known word.

This book will explore the mystery of OK: its odd origin, its unlikely survival, its varied forms and meanings, and its pervasive influence. OK is the most amazing invention in the history of American English.

The Everyday OK

It would not be much of an exaggeration to say that the modern world runs on OK (or plain lowercase *k*, if you are texting). We write those letters on documents to mark our approval. We speak them to express assent, or just to say we're listening. We accept a computer's actions by clicking on OK. And we also use OK to introduce matters of importance, or recall an audience's wandering attention.

Those are the simple obvious uses for OK, the ones we know well. In those situations, what a good friend OK is! A handy tool. An uncomplaining workhorse. Indeed, in America in the twenty-first century, it's hard to get through a conversation without a plentiful sprinkling of OK. It's the easiest way to signal agreement, whether with a written OK on a document or an OK spoken aloud:

OK, I'll go with you.

OK, you win.

At the start of a sentence, OK can also be a wakeup call, an alert, an attention getter, an announcement that something new is coming:

OK, I'll only say this once.

OK, I get it.

OK, let's start making our pinhole camera!

Blue Jeans, Shakespeare, and Light

To begin to grasp the full import of the phenomenon that is OK, we need to step back and consider it from fresh perspectives. When we do, we find that OK is like blue jeans, Shakespeare, and light.

Blue Jeans

OK is as American as jeans. In fact, it's very much like them. Nearly everyone uses both OK and jeans for everyday purposes, but not on formal occasions. And they are both American inventions of the nineteenth century that have spread to the far corners of the globe.

America's Shakespeare

Less obviously, OK is also America's answer to Shakespeare. Or more precisely, OK *is* America's Shakespeare, a two-letter expression as potent (though perhaps not as poetic) as anything in the Bard's works. Like Shakespeare, OK is protean, pervasive, influential, and successful in its own day and in ours. But the similarity goes deeper.

Like Shakespeare, OK had humble origins. This has set some critics on edge, prompting them to deny the attested origins in favor of more dignified ones.

For Shakespeare, the anti-Stratfordians reason that the "poacher from Stratford," a commoner, could not have written the noble language of Shakespeare's plays and poems. No, those works of genius must have come from a nobleman like the Earl of Oxford, a scholar like Francis Bacon, a college-educated playwright like Christopher Marlowe (whose death in 1593 must have been faked), or royalty—maybe Queen Elizabeth.

Similarly, for OK, elitists find it beyond embarrassing to think that OK began as a joke misspelling for "all correct." Surely, they reason, an expression as serious and important as OK must have come from a more serious abbreviation, like "Old Kinderhook" for presidential candidate Martin Van Buren in the 1840 election. Or maybe it came from baker Otto Kimmel's supposed custom of imprinting his initials in vanilla cookies. Or wait—maybe it was borrowed from another language, like Choctaw, Scottish, Greek, or Mandingo.

All very tempting, but overwhelming evidence shows otherwise.

Another thing OK and Shakespeare have in common is elusiveness. How do you properly spell OK? And is it a noun, verb, adjective, adverb, or interjection? Indeed, is it a word at all, an abbreviation, or something else? There are no simple answers to these questions.

Similarly, the text of Shakespeare's plays can't be pinned down. The quarto and folio versions of the plays published during or shortly after Shakespeare's lifetime have significant differences, and it is hard to imagine the full text of either quarto or folio being spoken quickly enough to fit the "two hours traffic" stated in the prologue to *Romeo and Juliet*.

Light

And light! Yes, OK is like light, in our post-Einsteinian understanding of that pervasive phenomenon. Before Einstein, physicists were puzzled: light sometimes appears to be a particle, sometimes a wave. Is light a wave or particle? Einstein's answer was "Yes, it's either, or both." That's the answer we have to give to the OK phenomenon. Is it a word or an abbreviation? Is it noun, verb, adjective, adverb, interjection, or all of the above? The answer has to be "Yes, it's either, or both, or all." It's an old-fashioned joke with a postmodern punch line.

So it will take a village of chapters to approach the heart of the mystery of OK.

The Many Spellings of OK

The elusiveness of OK begins with its first impression, its look on the page. OK has not one but many spellings. That's odd, when you think about it. Most words have just one acceptable spelling, though they may have varying pronunciation. OK, on the other hand, has just one pronunciation, the names of the letters O and K. Since it just consists of those two letters of the alphabet, why shouldn't there be just one spelling?

Well, it turns out that there are different ways to spell those two letters, and there is no consensus on which is the best. It can be *OK* in capital letters or *ok* in small. Either of those versions can be served plain or peppered with periods (*O.K., o.k.*), so those two letters make four more possibilities—or six, if we allow a space after the first period (*O. K., o. k.*).

If we're texting instead of talking, the shorter and simpler *k* rules. In a *New Yorker* review of a book on text messaging, Louis Menand declares, "The most common text message must be 'k.' It means 'I have nothing to say, but God forbid that you should think that I am ignoring your message.'" The medium is new, and so is that abbreviation, but not the message; a century and a half earlier, OK served a similar function in telegraphy, confirming that a message had been properly received.

Of course, the variation in spelling doesn't stop there. If we think of OK as a word, why shouldn't it be spelled like an ordinary word? In ordinary writing, when we aren't texting, we don't use

MLE for *Emily,* DK for *decay,* or TDS for *tedious.* So it is more conventional and less conspicuous to render OK as *okay* (or occasionally *okeh* or *okey*).

But suppose we opt for *okay.* Even that, it turns out, is not the expected spelling for a word pronounced OK. The problem is the *k.* English spelling does have some rules, chaotic as it often seems. One of the rules is to spell the *k* sound, when possible, with a *c.*

Before a vowel, we do spell the *k* sound with *k* if the vowel that follows is *e, i,* or *y.* That's to avoid mispronouncing a word with a soft *c* (an *s* or *ch*) sound, as in *circus* or *cello.* The spelling *c* is ambiguous before those vowels, so we allow *k.*

But when the vowel following the *k* sound is *a, o,* or *u,* there is no such ambiguity. In those cases, English spelling prefers *c,* not *k.* So the dictionary spells the names of certain plants as *oca* and *ocotillo,* not *oka* and *okotillo.* We write *oculist,* not *okulist.*

True, *okay* is generally (though not always) spoken with emphasis on the second syllable, not the first as in those examples. In that case, the typical spelling for the *k* sound is a double *c,* as in *occult, occur,* and *occasion.* That last word happens to begin with the exact same sounds as OK. For some reason, however, we don't spell OK as *occay.*

Why don't we notice that the spelling *okay* is odd? Two reasons. First, we're so used to *okay* that we don't question it. It has had that spelling for nearly a century and a half. And second, it does follow a certain logic, however exceptional. There's a *k* in the two-letter versions of OK, so a spelling that starts out *ok-* is more closely connected to its sibling than one that begins *oc-.* Further, the name of the letter *k* takes the exceptional spelling *kay,* making the connection to the two-letter spelling even closer. That's different from the expected spelling *cay,* referring to a little island of sand or coral.

So *okay* is an odd yet logical spelling, following a different drummer than most words with the *k* sound before the vowel *a*.

Konspikuous Ks

In the English alphabet, no letter is more conspicuous than *k*. Or to put it another way, no letter has a better ready-made opportunity to be conspicuous than *k*. That's because, thanks to the versatility of *c, k* really isn't needed in English. It was a late addition to the English alphabet, used regularly in English writing only after the Norman conquest, a mere thousand years ago.

So *k* makes OK stand out. Indeed, with regard to recent borrowings into English of foreign words beginning with "non-English initial combinations" like *ka-*, the *Oxford English Dictionary* says that these spellings suggest "the uncouth or barbarous character of the words."

In all its spelling variations, OK makes use of the conspicuous letter *k,* instead of the correct and less conspicuous *c.* Other words take advantage of the power of *k* too: *K* for *strikeout* in baseball, even though it's not the initial letter, *KO* for a *knockout* in boxing (a twentieth-century innovation possibly suggested by being a simple reversal of OK), even though it's a silent letter, and two Ks in *Kodak*, deliberately chosen to make that name distinctive.

Many Parts of Speech

Adjective First

When we turn from spelling to grammar, the hydra-headedness of OK continues. It won't be confined to a single part of speech. In fact, OK fits every one of the four major grammatical categories:

noun, verb, adjective, and adverb, as well as the wild-card category
of interjection.

At heart, OK is an adjective, modifying a noun. It was that
way in its very first appearance, in a Boston newspaper in 1839,
and it has thrived that way ever since. To take a few examples
plucked from the Web:

> **Finding flaws on our website is OK.**
>
> **Gwyneth's Marriage Is OK, Says Mom (headline)**
>
> **We Are Not Perfect, but We Are OK (title of a human
> anatomy exhibit)**

This is OK as a predicate adjective, coming after the noun it
modifies as well as the verb of the sentence (most often *is*). It's one
of two common positions in a sentence for an adjective. The other
is right before the noun, what's known as an attributive adjective,
and OK readily assumes that position too.

> **Burris will be at least an OK U.S. senator, probably a decent
> one and maybe even a good one. (*Chicago Tribune*)**

Noun, Verb, Adverb

But OK was too versatile to be limited to its original part of speech
as an adjective. Sometimes it became a thing, taking on the form
and function of a noun. The form includes the possibility of a
plural, and the function includes object and subject of a sentence,
as well as object of a preposition, all illustrated in the first of these
examples:

> **He includes another boxed and starred "OK," but he does not
> silently write it, as before. This "OK" is not primarily iconic**

but orally expressive, like the "OKs" of his homework story. (*Handbook of Early Literacy Research*)

Sounds to me her English level was not so high, so her OK was simply a way of acknowledging his statement.

When this OK becomes our everyday attitude, when we accept reality, we can at last live in the middle of reality.

What else? Well, you can verb OK easily enough, adding the inflections *-s, -ed,* and *-ing* as appropriate. It occurs especially in newspaper headlines, where OK is attractive to editors because it takes up less space than *approve* or another alternative:

Phillips Says She OK'd Use of Photo

Woman Admits She OK'd Fraudulent Loan

L.A. Council OKs 3-Month Moratorium on Billboards

Council OKs Smoking Pot in WAMM Tent

Less common, but still plentiful, is OK as an adverb, modifying a verb or an entire sentence. Here is an example, embedded in a 1954 letter by Chicago newspaperman Mike Royko to his future wife:

This caused the officer in charge of my section to feel that I had put a black mark on his record so he gave me a long winded lecture. I took the lecture OK but when he asked me if I planned on reenlisting I blew my stack.

Interjection!

Finally, there is OK the interjection, the wild card located in a third dimension outside the structure of the rest of the sentence. It's perhaps the most common use for OK nowadays:

OK, show me the money.

OK, I give up. What's the answer?

OK, what is this Venus retrograde all about?

And being unrelated grammatically to anything else in the sentence, the interjection OK can also occur all by itself. Or merely be repeated, as in the song from a 2007 album by the Swedish group the Bombhappies with the title *Ok ok ok ok ok ok ok*, or Juliana Hatfield's song "OK, OK," from her 1995 album "Only Everything," with the chorus

> OK OK, whatever you say.
> OK OK, I did it but I didn't.
> OK OK, don't make me get crazy.
> OK OK OK OK, OK, OK.

To give the interjection an emphatic positive spin, you can add an exclamation point to make it OK! (which happens to be the title of a celebrity magazine, first published in Britain and recently also available in an American edition).

The Wordhood of OK

The multiplicity of spellings and grammatical uses leads to a more fundamental question: What is OK, anyway? Is it a word? If so, why do we spell it OK, like an abbreviation or acronym? Or is it an abbreviation or acronym? If so, why do we spell it *okay*? And if an abbreviation, what does it stand for?

There's a simple answer, but it's not fully satisfying. Simply stated, OK is an abbreviation, an acronym, technically an initialism— the name of each initial letter sounded— for *all correct*. And yes, the perpetrator knew that the initials were not correct at all.

That's how OK began. But it wasn't long before the ridiculous abbreviation was forgotten and fanciful false explanations of its origin began to emerge in its place. Though the true origin of OK was uncovered and exhaustively demonstrated by Columbia University professor Allen Walker Read nearly fifty years ago, it's safe to say that hardly any one of the many millions who use it nowadays knows what OK originally stood for.

If we consider OK an initialism, it would be in the same class as IOU, FBI, USA, or more recent abbreviations like FAQ, IMHO, ROFL, WTF. If we consider OK a word, it's like *scuba* (self-contained underwater breathing apparatus) or *laser* (light amplification by stimulated emission of radiation).

But either way it's the dunce in the class, the pseudo-ignorant fool with a sign pinned to its back proclaiming its failure to master even the rudiments of proper spelling. It might seem good to let its origin remain obscure so that the grown-up OK can go about its serious business nowadays without evoking laughter. But it's all the more impressive when we recognize its triumphant ascent from humble beginnings.

The Meaning of OK: The Neutral Affirmer

Amidst its many spellings and grammatical uses, OK manages to retain the essence of the definition it was given at its birth: "all correct." It affirms. An action succeeds, a device works, and a person survives if they are OK. If a document is OK, it is approved. If food is OK, you can eat it. If your car is OK, you can drive it without worry. If a patient in a hospital is OK, you can expect that the person will recover. If you click an OK box on your computer, you approve of what it's doing. If a friend answers "OK" when you propose a change in plans, you know the change is approved.

As long as it is in an either-or situation, OK is as positive as can be. OK is as good as it gets when you accept an offer, confirm an arrival, or proofread a page. Typically in this situation OK is used as an interjection, either by itself or leading off a sentence. Or it's an interjection at the end of a sentence, asking for confirmation. Maybe you're confirming plans with someone:

> OK, we'll meet at 10 a.m. this Saturday at Anne's house on 123 Main Street. Can you be in charge of bringing extra pens?

> I'm coming home now, OK? OK, see you in a bit.

Or more simply, an exchange sometimes repeated several times at the end of a discussion,

> OK? OK.

But even in those situations, OK affirms without evaluating. That plans have been made and accepted is certain. Whether that is welcome or grudging, OK doesn't say. You have to add a quali-fying word or phrase to make that clear:

> OK, great! We'll meet at 10 a.m. this Saturday. . . .

> OK, that will really ruin the weekend, but if we have to, we'll meet at 10 a.m. this Saturday. . . .

If it's OK, it's all correct. But it's not necessarily wonderful. Or terrible either. About the value of the affirmation, OK just doesn't say. No wonder it is so useful.

In its earliest days, especially during the presidential campaign of 1840, when OK was just a year old, OK could express enthusi-asm. Tammany OK Clubs boisterously supported the reelection of incumbent Martin Van Buren. (He still lost.) But the vigor injected into OK by the election of 1840 did not spread to every instance of its use. Even back then OK had the distinctive quality of today's basic meaning: affirming without evaluating. As far back as 1872, Maximilian Schele de Vere wrote in his book *Americanisms*, "To the question how a convalescent is, the answer comes back: "Oh, he is quite O. K. again!" OK wasn't enough of an affirmation; he needed *quite* as well.

Here are more examples of an OK that isn't so wonderful:

Just these few lines to tell you I got here all O.K. but I left my coat in the ladies dressing room in Los Angeles. (Letter from Josephine Earp to her husband, Wyatt, in 1929)

Well Bud how are you and the folks? O.K. I hope. I am well and getting along fairly well still working in the shirt shop. (Letter from bank robber John Dillinger, in jail, to his brother in 1930)

You can apply the *very* test to see how noncommittal OK is. Most adjectives can express greater intensity with the modifying adverb *very*, as in *very good* or *very satisfying*. But you can't say *very OK*; something is either simply OK or not. The prohibition extends to all modifying adverbs, so we never (or hardly ever) say *extremely OK*, *thoroughly OK*, *moderately OK*, *partly OK*, or the like.

Furthermore, unlike most other adjectives, OK refuses to allow comparatives or superlatives: you can say *better*, *best*, or *more satisfying*, *most satisfying*, but not *OKer*, *OKest*, or *more OK*, *most OK*.

So by itself, OK is value neutral. Whenever there are different degrees of acceptability, OK doesn't point to any particular one. By default, that permits mediocrity as well as excellence. OK is not a sufficiently positive response to questions like "How do I look?" or "What did you think of my dinner?" Used that way, OK can deflate a balloon—or anything else. Some examples from the Web:

> Yes, it was an OK balloon, but I wanted a bigger one.

> This vacuum did an OK job. Don't expect superior cleaning with this one.

> Went to Peasant last nite and had great food. The decor is OK, the service OK but the food is wonderful!

> In terms of the chicken the most we can say is that it was OK. OK meaning not lousy and not spectacular either. It was OK as in good OK but not exceptional that we'd rave about it.

Regarding the relatively disappointing reception for Michael Jackson's 2001 album *Invincible*, a commentator on VH1 said,

> In the end, it was an OK record. And nobody was interested in OK for Michael Jackson.

In Oklahoma, the OK Chorale (named for the state) is a serious award-winning barbershop group. But outside Oklahoma, a chorus that puts OK in front of its name makes a point of its mediocrity. The OK Chorale of Seattle, Washington, declares:

> The OK Chorale is an ASUW [Associated Students of the University of Washington] Experimental College non-audition choir of folks who love to sing. We sing in 4-part harmony and have experienced singers and uncertain beginners, music readers and non-readers. The rehearsals are fun and no one gets hurt. Just because your grade school music teacher told you to mouth the words is no reason not to sing out now.

Likewise, in Boston there is the OK Chorale, a filk/folk chorus. And what is filk? According to Jordin Kare in *Sing Out!* magazine:

> Filkers are, by tradition, extremely bad singers, and many filksongs parody filking itself. The traditional filkish key is Off, and a classic filk chorus starts, "So belt out whatever note suits you / The rest will join in, each one in his own key. . . ."

How negative OK can become is illustrated by one of the Nine Most Widely Used Words by Women on David Tan's website:

> (6) That's Okay: This is one of the most dangerous statements a woman can make to a man. *That's okay* means she wants to think long and hard before deciding how and when you will pay for your mistake.

Another Meaning: The Lecturer's OK

> Carmody clears her throat. She says, "Stay right where you are, please. Stop." Her voice is loud enough for them to hear, but it is not demanding.
>
> The young woman reaches out on each side of her, grabbing a hand of each of the men. Her lips move.
>
> Carmody thinks the girl said, "Okay." She imagines the word in her head and decides that the girl didn't mean "okay" as in "good." She meant "okay" as in "now."
>
> The trio begins to move forward. . . . (Stephen White, *The Siege* [2009], 124)

This example from a novel reflects what many of us do in conversation: use OK as a "structural marker," not so much to affirm as to introduce, punctuate, or conclude what we have to say. In some people's speech OK even serves as a filler word, equivalent to *you know*, *like*, *uh*, or *um*. Speakers use fillers to avoid silence while they are thinking of what to say next, because silence would invite interruption.

One frequent modern use of OK is what Harry Levin and Deborah Gray called "the lecturer's OK," as in, "OK. The final study I'm going to talk about had to do with. . . ." It's a natural spin-off from the simple affirmative interjection at the start of a sentence, the OK of "OK, I'll meet you there in ten minutes." We are so used to beginning a sentence with that interjection that it easily is picked up to introduce a new topic or just call for our attention. Indeed, sometimes it calls to attention the speaker more than the listener; some people will say OK to themselves as they review points they want to make. (Or they may say *all right*, the closest synonym of OK, as Erik Schleef recently pointed out.)

The Old Philosophy of OK: Making It Work

Alexis de Tocqueville, writing around the time of the birth of OK, could make the argument that Americans have no philosophy. They are too pragmatic; they just go about their business.

Perhaps so. But if there is an American philosophy, it could be argued that it is simply OK.

That OK should embody a philosophy seems, at first glance, absurd. Two letters born of a joke and used for practical purposes hardly make a view of life or a guiding principle. In fact, to this day formal philosophical discourse, like all formal discourse, generally avoids using OK at all.

But it could be argued that OK is the American philosophy, expressing in two letters our pragmatism, our efficiency, our concern to get things accomplished by hook or crook. We don't insist that everything be perfect; OK is good enough, and much better than not OK.

It has been said that democracy is the worst form of government, except for everything else. Similarly, OK is the worst way of getting along, except for everything else. As Tim Gunn says, make it work! With OK, it does. In the words of the moral of a short story by humorist George Ade, one of the popularizers of OK early in the twentieth century:

Any System is O.K. if it finally Works Out.

The New Philosophy of OK: I'm OK—You're OK

Beginning in the 1960s, and thanks to that one famous OK quotation, another philosophy of OK began to spread. It was one of tolerance and acceptance, as in these recent postings on the Web:

It's OK to wear what you want.

It's OK to choose melodies where only a line or two are immediately singable by the congregation.

It's OK to choose not to vaccinate your kids.

It's OK not to have a child. It's OK to adopt or foster. It's OK to make choices your mother won't understand.

If you don't know what you want to major in, you are not alone. Many freshmen and sophomores haven't picked a major yet. And guess what? That's OK.

It would be a mistake to claim that OK caused the American philosophies of pragmatism in the nineteenth century and tolerance in the twentieth. But OK has become an expression of both—a concise, poignant, and constant reminder.

OK as a touchstone for tolerance goes back to that best-selling book published in 1967: *I'm OK, You're OK* by Thomas Harris. The book was about the kind of psychology known as transactional analysis, first popularized by Eric Berne's 1964 book *Games People Play*. The particulars of transactional analysis have faded from public awareness, but the simplified message conveyed by Harris's title thrives as a basis for present-day tolerance of diversity and hence acceptance of self. Thanks to that title, the two letters OK have acquired the power to make us feel good about ourselves, deserving or not.

That's relatively new territory for OK. It was around for more than a century before Harris's book gave it a new spin. And *I'm OK, You're OK* couldn't have happened to an ordinary word. But OK is anything but ordinary in its form and in its history.

The OK Taboo

O.K. (or *OK* or *okay*) is widely used on every level of speech and on all levels of writing except the stodgiest. Unless you are taking freshman English, you can use it freely.

—*Merriam-Webster's Concise Dictionary of English Usage*

OK has so many oddities that it is hard to tell which is the oddest. But a leading candidate for oddest, surely, is the taboo against using OK, or even its more conventional respelling *okay*, in formal discourse.

When OK first appeared, it must have seemed not quite suitable for polite company. It wasn't sacrilegious or obscene, like certain other four-letter words that even nowadays are banned from broadcast. But it did have low associations, with people (purely hypothetical) whose knowledge of spelling was so poor that they would actually spell "all correct" *oll korrect*, and also with the rowdy Tammany ruffians of the OK Clubs in the 1840 election.

It had the stigma of slang, not for what it meant or how it was pronounced but because it was a deliberately blatant, stupid misspelling. As such, it was attributed, in jest or otherwise, to ignorant people, to be avoided by those who wanted to be considered cultured.

Whatever the reason, OK never made it to the pages of most of the better nineteenth-century authors. It's not surprising that you won't find OK in the works of, say, Henry James. But it's not even used by Mark Twain and Bret Harte, who wrote about low characters and used their slang. And when OK slipped once into the works of Henry David Thoreau and Louisa May Alcott, it was removed in subsequent editions.

That's no longer the case. The dialogue used by many authors of the twentieth and twenty-first centuries freely includes OK. And though it has a lengthy entry in the recent *Historical Dictionary of American Slang*, few people nowadays think of it as slang. Nevertheless, despite its ubiquity, it remains strictly excluded from whole genres and many books.

You will look in vain through the inaugural addresses of the presidents of the United States, even as informal a president as George W. Bush, for a single instance of OK. Similarly, you can page through volume after volume of scholarly publications without turning up an OK, except in reports of conversations.

To take a more extreme example, consider the Bible. In more than three-quarters of a million words, OK doesn't show up even once in most English versions.

You wouldn't find OK in the original Hebrew and Greek, of course. Nor could OK have appeared in the King James Version, published in 1611, more than two hundred years before the invention of OK. But there are now many contemporary English translations, including ones in colloquial language, and they too avoid OK.

There's one exception, the colloquial translation called *The Message*. But even it has only one OK from the entire Hebrew Bible and only one, repeated once, from the New Testament, both in dialogue:

> "I don't care; let me run." "Okay," said Joab, "run." So Ahimaaz ran. . . . (2 Samuel 18:23)

> The voice came a second time: "If God says it's okay, it's okay." (Acts 10:15)

> "Then I heard a voice: 'Go to it, Peter—kill and eat.' I said, 'Oh, no, Master. I've never so much as tasted food that wasn't kosher.' The voice spoke again: 'If God says it's okay, it's okay. . . .'" (Acts 11:7)

A more conventional translation of the latter, from the New International Version, is "Do not call anything impure that God has made clean."

There's no mystery why OK isn't often employed in the Bible. Aside from being insufficiently dignified, it's too neutral. Imagine the story of the Creation in the Hebrew Bible with OK instead of "very good":

> And God saw every thing that he had made, and, behold, it was OK. And the evening and the morning were the sixth day. (Genesis 1:31)

The Presidential OK

Because we hesitate to use OK in formal situations, it's rare to find it in a presidential speech on a serious issue, but it's not impossible. Here are a few examples from Barack Obama's public speaking. He used OK in speaking to schoolchildren on September 8, 2009:

> But the truth is, being successful is hard. You won't love every subject you study. You won't click with every teacher. Not every homework assignment will seem completely relevant to your life right this minute. And you won't necessarily succeed at everything the first time you try.
>
> That's OK. Some of the most successful people in the world are the ones who've had the most failures.

Generally, however, official presidential OKs are few and far between. It is only when speaking informally that OK occurs in the transcripts of President Obama's remarks. Interrupted at a rally on health insurance reform at the University of Maryland on September 17, 2009, he said, according to the official transcript,

> (audience interruption) What's going on, guys? We're doing OK. Relax. Everybody is all right. We're doing fine. (Applause)

And later in that speech:

> You just heard Rachel's story. She's OK right now, she's thriving.

At a joint press conference with Canadian prime minister Stephen Harper on September 16, 2009, President Obama opened the questioning with this:

> OK. All right, Ben Feller.

Later that month, finishing a press conference at the G20 sum-
mit meeting in Pittsburgh, he used OK to make sure there were no
more questions:

**OK? Thank you very much, everybody. I hope you enjoy
Pittsburgh.**

The Word That Shouldn't Have Been Born

OK. Now, think for a moment of a world without OK. By all
odds, that should be the world we inhabit. Maybe the oddest thing
about OK is its mere existence.

OK wasn't needed. It wasn't animal, vegetable, or mineral, no
newly discovered ocelot, okra, or obsidian requiring a name. It
wasn't a new product or invention, neither reaping machine nor
revolver. It was nothing concrete in need of a label, neither lapdog
or laptop. Nor was it an abstract political or philosophical concept
like democracy or deconstruction. *All right* was already at hand to
express the essential meaning of OK. In short, our language
needed OK as much as a fish needs a bicycle, to use a famous
comparison.

Before its invention, it would not have appeared on anyone's list
of needed words, the list that nowadays includes a term for "brothers and sisters" that isn't as formal as *siblings*, and a gender-neutral
personal pronoun to replace *he* or *she*. And yet, when created almost
by happenstance, it caught on, better than most creations.

The Word That Shouldn't Have Lived

As anyone who has tried it knows, inventing a word is no guaran-
tee that anyone else will use it, let alone that it will be enshrined in

dictionaries. And as anyone who has tried it knows, the more conspicuous an invented word, the less likely it is to be taken up into the vocabulary. And OK is, and was, conspicuous.

It's not just that it began as a joke. True, our language has other initialisms like IOU and PDQ, not to mention more modern abbreviations like NIMBY and ROFL. But those are different; their spelling is OK. In contrast, for most of its first seventy years or so, OK was well known to be a blatant misspelling of "all correct."

It's hard enough for a normal-looking word to gain acceptance into our vocabulary, but for such an oddity as OK, the odds would seem to be almost impossible. It doesn't fit the mold of words we admit to the English language. In fact, it breaks the mold.

Words generally come into being by evolution, not special creation. Most new words come from old ones naturally developing new meanings or combining in new ways, rather than from conscious invention. Even experts at inventing new words usually fall flat. As examples of conscious and conspicuous coinage, who could forget humorist Gelett Burgess's *cowcat,* meaning an insignificant person? Or futurist Faith Popcorn's *blanquilized*, meaning a person "so loaded up with tranquilizers that they go through the day in a medicinal fog"? As is turns out, just about everyone has forgotten these artificial coinages, or never used them in the first place.

As a rule, oddities die out. Words conspicuous for their odd shape or for their cleverness rarely last longer than a round of chuckles. We may enjoy them, but we don't adopt them into our vocabulary, just as we wouldn't invite a circus menagerie into our home. And indeed, the numerous equally odd misspelled cousins of newborn OK, expressions like *o.w.* for *all right, k.y.* for *no use,* and *n.s.m.g.* for *enough said among gentlemen,* vanished as soon as the short-lived fad for abbreviations faded.

But OK had luck on its side. It managed not just to survive but to flourish in its infancy. And with that strong beginning, in less than a century it developed into America's greatest invention.

Fertile Soil

OK certainly falls in the category of conspicuous coinage. Where conspicuousness usually dooms a neologism, this most conspicuous word made a virtue of its bizarreness and thrived because of its oddity rather than despite it.

So how did it survive?

Once it was launched, conditions had to be just right for the propagation of OK . . . but they were. OK was able to establish itself because of four unique circumstances in its early years:

1. The fad for joking abbreviations in Boston newspapers of the late 1830s

2. The campaign for reelection of a United States president who happened to come from Kinderhook, New York

3. Former President Andrew Jackson's humble origins

4. The invention of the telegraph

The unlikely coincidence of these four circumstances created the perfect storm that allowed OK to flourish during the nineteenth century, both in practical use and as a marginalized slang term. It remained for the early twentieth century to rescue OK from the margin so that it could be used as widely as it is today. Perhaps the key impetus for that modern development was the almost universal amnesia about the true origins of OK that took place early in the twentieth century. With the source of OK forgotten, each ethnic group and tribe could claim the honor of having ushered it into being from an expression in their native language. With pride in OK thus replacing embarrassment about using it, OK settled into its current respectable maturity.

That's how it is today. The next chapter tells how it began.

A SATURDAY
MORNING
IN BOSTON

ON SATURDAY, MARCH 23, 1839, A VISITOR TO BOSTON might have picked up a copy of that day's *Boston Morning Post* and chanced upon this item in the second column on the second page, a report from Providence, Rhode Island:

> Quite an excitement was caused here [in Providence] yesterday, by an announcement in the Boston Post, that a deputation from the Boston A. B. R. S. would pass through the city, on their way to N. York. Nothing but the short notice prevented the Marine Artillery from turning out to do honor to the occasion. The report proved unfounded, however, and has led to the opinion here that the Post is not the *organ* of that illustrious body.

ecision were these :—Mr
had moved an amendment
kley, of Barnstable, moved
ndment—and to this sec-
er, of Otis, moved another
and last amendment, the
of order, and the rule laid
ach occasions was perfectly
amendment to an amend-
at, but that, as this rule, if
t, would cause confusion,
universal custom that it
er than the amendment to
e Speaker read the rule in
.87, 88, which was perfect-
ny blame was to be at-
tion, it must be shared with

ned the Chair, Mr CHASE,
nsideration of the vote of
the minimum of three gal-
one gallon. A long and
a which the member from
: "legislated for a wife and
d some personalities at the
Lancaster, who was called
Springfield, and checked
ion of the question was
and nays ordered on the
the words "one gallon."
the motion to re-consider
 native—Yeas, 228—Nays,
he House then adjourned
entertaining any motion to
ity.
gallons," was substituted
being taken by yeas and
207. The previous question
not sustained, and Mr
offered a very long amend-
very inaudible tone. Mr
ed the bill reported by the
as he called Mr Bliss and
de an animated speech in
S, which he would have
ohibition against the sale
ner as ardent spirits are

nan, spoke in reply to Mr
New Bedford, followed on
quence of the impatience
he gave way to a motion

time is near at hand when
sex must once more buckle
st to secure a member of
o. 4. Cheered on by the
they will come to the field
trong hands: let energy,
their action, and a tri-

—for Caleb to play with when he is n't doing *chores*
for the Governor. Apply at the Council Chamber.

☞ Quite an excitement was caused here yesterday, by an announcement in the Boston Post, that a
deputation from the Boston A. B. R. S. would pass
through the city, on their way to N. York. Nothing
but the short notice prevented the Marine Artillery
from turning out to do honor to the occasion. The
report proved unfounded, however, and has led to the
opinion here that the Post is not the *organ* of that
illustrious body.

The above is from the Providence Journal, the editor of which is a little too quick on the trigger, on
this occasion. We said not a word about our deputation passing "through the city" of Providence.—
We said our brethren were going to New York in the
Richmond, and they did go, as per Post of Thursday.
The "Chairman of the Committee on Charity Lecture Bells," is one of the deputation, and perhaps if
he should return to Boston, via Providence, he of
the Journal, and his *train*-band, would have the
"contribution box," et ceteras, *o. k.*—all correct—and
cause the corks to fly, like *sparks,* upward.

Forgeries.—We learn that a large number of forgeries, amounting to several thousands of dollars, were
detected yesterday at the banks in this town. The
perpetrator, a young man of respectable connections,
and who has hitherto sustained an irreproachable
character, left here several days since, and was last
seen in New York, on his way south.—*N. Bedford
Mercury.*

Hampden County.—The Hampden Post of the 20th
instant says—

"The town elections in this county so far as we
have received returns, have resulted favorably to the
democratic cause. Granville and Monson, two federal towns last autumn, have, we understand elected
democratic town officers this spring by very decided
majorities. This is highly encouraging. Let other
towns follow the example. Palmer and Westfield
maintain their strong democratic majorities."

Tit for Tat.—The Nashua Gazette—one of the best
democratic papers we receive—contains the following
clever squib :—

"The Telegraph says a person was bailed out of
Amherst jail to vote the democratic ticket. Indeed !
What was the "whig," who was put there for par-
ticipation in the same affair bailed out for ?'

The Whigs elected N. B. Borden, Moderator of
their Town Meeting, at Fall River, on Monday last.
This is the man who pretended to be a democrat as
long as the democrats would send him to Congress to
vote against them.

☞ Mr Brownson's Discourse to-morrow morning, at the Masonic Temple, we are told will be on
TRANSUBSTANTIATION.

☞ *On the First Page*—Poetry—The Oratorio of
David—The Wisdom and Genius of Shakspeare—
The Irish Charitable Society's Anniversary Celebra-
tion—Burning the President in effigy, &c.

---

iffs, printers and other accou
Bills passed to be enacted-
Congregational Society in D
corporate the Wardens, V
Christ Church in Springfield
The Secretary of the Com
the following message from
To the Senate and House of
I transmit to the two Hou
ceived yesterday, from His
of Maine, of the 19th inst.,
Resolutions of the Legislatu
priating the sum of $10,000
from Houlton to the Aroosto
a like appropriation on the p
E
Council Chamber, 22d Ma
This Message was read a
mittee on Public Lands.
The House then proceede
the License Bill, and on m
lem, the vote whereby the
to strike out the word one, w
question then recurring on
setting three, it was divide
nays, and the first part there
ative, yeas 228, nays 216,
question, the House adjourn
Afternoon.—Bill passed to
construction of the Western
Sundry papers from the S
The House proceeded to t
resumed the consideration o
sale of spirituous liquors.
question pending at the last
the insertion of the word "th
proviso of the first section,
second section was taken
decided in the affirmative, 2
Mr Hinckley, of Barnstable,
the proviso of the first sect
5th and 6th sections, and
House adjourned.

☞ Dr Bartlett opened his
lative Committee, yesterday
quent and forcible plea.
again this morning at 8 o'cle
Sprague as counsel for the
Hallett for Dr Bartlett.

☞ Our series of "Sketc
which have been suspended
room for the proceedings in
the license law, will be resu
itinued till the close of the
sired event should not be po
4th of July.

How now ?—Col. Thayer,
to speak on the license bill, t
afternoon, "and is n't that a

Duel.—The Nashville Whi
near Moscow, Fayette cour
since, between Andrew Jack
vate secretary of Ex-Preside
Robinson—both slightly wou

"*Suffer little children to com
Augusta, Geo., on the 17th i
son, Mr Hiram Dill, aged 1

The above is from the Providence Journal, the editor of which is a little too quick on the trigger, on this occasion. We said not a word about our deputation passing "through the city" of Providence.—We said our brethren were going to New York in the Richmond, and they did go, as per Post of Thursday. The "Chairman of the Committee on Charity Lecture Bells," is one of the deputation, and perhaps if he should return to Boston, via Providence, he of the Journal, and his *train*-band, would have the "contribution box," et ceteras, *o. k.*—all correct—and cause the corks to fly, like *sparks*, upward.

What's all that? Frankly, a visitor from out of town might be as perplexed as we are today about the A.B.R.S. and the Boston paper's dispute with the *Providence Journal*. The visitor might well have stopped halfway through that item and moved on to the next:

> *Forgeries.*—We learn that a large number of forgeries, amounting to several thousands of dollars, were detected yesterday at the banks in this town. The perpetrator, a young man of respectable connections, and who has hitherto sustained an irreproachable character, left here several days since, and was last seen in New York, on his way south.—*N. Bedford Mercury.*

And continuing down the column:

> *Hampden County.*—The Hampden Post of the 20th instant says—
>
> "The town elections in this county so far as we have received returns, have resulted favorably to the democratic cause. [The *Morning Post* was very favorable to the Democratic Party, and so, most likely, would have been its readers.] Granville and

Monson, two federal towns last autumn, have, we understand elected democratic town officers this spring by very decided majorities. This is highly encouraging. Let other towns follow the example. Palmer and Westfield maintain their strong democratic majorities."

And so on through other pro-Democratic reports to:

Mr. Brownson's Discourse to-morrow morning, at the Masonic Temple, we are told will be on TRANSUBSTANTIATION.

On the First Page—Poetry—The Oratorio of David—The Wisdom and Genius of Shakespeare—The Irish Charitable Society's Anniversary Celebration—Burning the President in effigy, & c.

If with that encouragement the visitor turned back to the first page, that reader would have missed the humble birth of what would later prove to be the greatest American expression of all time—*o. k.*, coming at the end of the A.B.R.S. report quoted above. It's buried in that complicated last sentence:

. . . perhaps if he should return to Boston, via Providence, he of the Journal, and his *train*-band, would have the "contribution box," et ceteras, *o. k.*—all correct—and cause the corks to fly, like *sparks*, upward.

Even if it was not born in a stable, *o. k.* was anything but great in this first appearance. It appeared in lowercase letters, befitting its lowly employment as an attempt at humor (and also not abbreviating a proper noun). The joke that *o. k.* would be an abbreviation for *all correct*, when neither *o* nor *k* was the correct spelling, was such a stretch that it required the explanation "*o. k.*—all correct" to follow immediately.

Only a faithful reader of the *Morning Post* would have been able to disentangle the complicated comments leading up to the attempt at humor of *o. k.* Fortunately, linguistic historian Allen Walker Read patiently read through many issues of the *Morning Post* and other newspapers of the time to provide an explanation for modern readers.

It seems that A.B.R.S. stands for "Anti-Bell-Ringing Society." In the previous year, among other business, the Boston Common Council had issued an ordinance prohibiting the ringing of dinner bells. In response, in October 1838 a number of men jokingly formed the A.B.R.S., not to support the ordinance, as "Anti-Bell-Ringing" might suggest, but to oppose it. As soon as the A.B.R.S. was founded, the *Morning Post* began to chronicle its activities, summarizing its purpose in the issue of January 7, 1839, a few months before the birth of *o. k.*:

> The main design of the founders of the Society was and is, to expose and oppose, by ridicule and otherwise, the spirit of ultraism in legislation, which is so prevailing a characteristic of the present time.

Among the officials of the A.B.R.S., as Read notes, were "Chief Butler and Imperturbable Deliberator," "Confabulator, to do all the Society's Unnecessary Talking," and "Professor of Bell-ocution." And so in that spirit, two days before the first appearance of *o. k.*, the *Boston Morning Post* announced:

> A.B.R.S.—We understand that a large deputation from this society will take passage in the John W. Richmond steamer for New York to-day, for the purpose of extending friendly congratulations with the auxiliary society in the Commercial Emporium. [In contrast, Boston was known as the Literary Emporium.]

That was the background for the appearance of *o. k.* in the report quoted at the beginning of this chapter. The *Providence Daily Journal* supposed that the A.B.R.S. would make an appearance in Providence, but as the *Boston Morning Post* noted in its response, "We said not a word about our deputation passing 'through the city' of Providence." But the *Post* concludes its March 23 commentary by imagining the festivities that would occur if the A.B.R.S. made an appearance, "all correct."

It was a typical issue of the *Boston Morning Post* for 1839, a single sheet folded to make four 16-by-26-inch pages of small print, beginning with advertising classified under headings like these:

BUSINESS CARDS.

BOOKS AND STATIONARY [*sic*].

AUCTION SALES.

DISEASED SPINES.

COMMERCIAL.

MARINE JOURNAL.

TREMONT THEATRE.

NATIONAL THEATRE.

The back page was filled with advertising for dry goods, railroads (complete with schedules), and medical remedies, such as

Dr. Gordak's Jelly of Pomegranate and Peruvian Pills, highly recommended for Nervous Headache, Dizziness in the Head, Palpitation of the Heart, Oppression of the Breast, Dyspepsia, Flatulency, Costiveness, Darting pains in the Side, Back, and Limbs, most efficacious for Jaundice and Liver-complaint, most valuable for Blind and Bleeding Piles, for impurities of

the Blood as Salt Rheum, Scrofula, Erysipelas, Tellers and
Cancer, it is positively the best Medicine ever invented. It is
also unrivalled in colds, coughs, and catarrh.

At this time the *Morning Post* was less than a decade old, having been founded in 1831 by William Beals and Charles Gordon
Greene. It was already the city's leading newspaper, as it would
remain for the next century. And because Greene was the editor in
1839, known for his wit and his bantering with other newspapers,
it is almost certain that Greene himself was the father of *o. k.*

If anyone else had invented *o. k.*, it might well have been still-
born. In that first appearance, there wasn't much to recommend it
or foresee its future greatness. But Greene evidently liked his egregiously incorrect "all correct." He probably was responsible also
for the next instance of *o. k.*, published three days later in the *Post*.
It was purportedly a letter from Providence, dated on the same day
as the original *o. k.* in the *Post,* claiming that A.B.R.S. members did
in fact visit Providence, unbeknownst to the editor of the *Journal*.
The letter displays the penchant for abbreviation that favored
the birth of *o. k.* It begins with an allusion to the March 23 report
in the *Post*:

PROVIDENCE, MARCH 23, 1839

To the Editor of the Post.—The Editor of the Providence Journal, on Friday, denied that a delegation from the Boston
A.B.R.S. went to New York on Thursday; but Saturday's paper
acknowledges, on the authority of a person whose "information is beyond all question," that they were here and took their
departure as per Post.

Many of O.F.M. [Our First Men] and several *futcheons*
[meaning unknown] had the pleasure of taking these "interesting strangers" by the hand, and wishing them a speedy passage

to the Commercial Emporium. They were o. k. Where was the editor of the Journal? Is his paper the "*organ*" of the A.B.R.S.? Will he be informed of the precise time of their return, and have suitable preparations made for causing "the corks to fly, like sparks, upward"? Or will it be N.G. [no good]? . . .

So there it is, the second attested appearance of *o. k.*, this time already assumed to be familiar enough to readers of the *Post* that it needed no translation or italics. Maybe Greene had second thoughts about its familiarity, however. On April 10, 1839, he used it again, this time in capitals and with a double explanation:

> *A new tie-up for Bostonians.*—Mr. MICHAEL HUGHES, better known here by his well earned office of "Magnificent Punch Distiller for the A.B.R.S." has opened a new hotel in New York, 6 Rosevelt street, near Pearl and Chatham, under the name of the "New England House." It is hardly necessary to say to those who know Mr. Hughes, that his establishment will be found to be "A. No. One"—that is, O.K.—all correct.

This foreshadows the use of *AOK* more than a century later. OK hadn't yet become a household term in 1839, but Greene continued to use it occasionally, and by October it had spread to another Boston newspaper, the *Evening Transcript*:

> A GOOD OMEN. So little *excitement* has been created here by the suspension of the U.S. Bank and its dependencies, that our Bank Directors have not thought it worth their while to call a meeting, even for consultation, on the subject. It is o. k. (*all correct*) in this quarter. [October 11]

Meanwhile, in the summer of 1839, OK made its way to New York. On September 2, the *New York Evening Tattler* gave New York a taste of OK:

Carlyle.—We are told by the Mirror that *Carlyle,* author of "Sartor Resartus," is coming to America to lecture. Vell, vot ov it! He can't help making money; for all foreigners do that, when they come to America, whether humbugs or not. Aye! and then go home and abuse us for our credulity. These "wise men from the East," who came so far to enlighten our darkness, are right enough, of course, to play at bowls with us as long as we are willing to set ourselves up, like skittles, to be knocked down for their amusement and emolument. O K ! all correct!

Still in 1839, by November OK had spread to Philadelphia, in this report by the editor of the *Philadelphia Gazette* about the New York fad for abbreviations in his November 12 issue:

They have a curious, short-hand phraseology in Wall street which it is amusing to hear. A man offers another a note with the endorsement of a third,—and saying of it—"You see it's A. I., the man is decidedly O.F.M."
"Yes—that's good—O.K.—I.S.B.D." [it shall be done] . . .

This story, in turn, was reprinted in New York, Baltimore, and New Orleans within a month.

So it began, and once begun, there was no stopping OK. But how could it have begun? What motivated Charles Gordon Greene to "have the 'contribution box,' et ceteras, *o. k.*—all correct" in the first place?

It could only have happened because of the odd fad mentioned above. As Read explains, "Beginning in the summer of 1838, there developed in Boston a remarkable vogue of using abbreviations. It might well be called a craze." Greene may be the one who started it all. Read gives this example from the *Morning Post* of June 12, 1838:

> *Melancholy*—We understand that J. Eliot Brown, Esq., Secretary of the Boston Young Men's Society for Meliorating the Condition of the Indians, F.H.H. (fell at Hoboken, N.J.) on Saturday last at 4 o'clock, P.M. in a duel W.O.O.O.F.C. (with one of our first citizens). What measures will be taken by the Society in consequence of this heart rending event, R.T.B.S. (remains to be seen).

Greene also used, varying between capital letters and small caps, N.G. (no go), S.P. (small potatoes), G.C. (gin cocktail), M.J. (mint julep), and G.T. (gone to Texas—to escape the jurisdiction of the United States).

These initialisms are not so different from those used in Internet chat today, like BTW (by the way), LOL (laughing out loud), and IMHO (in my humble opinion). Greene's on-the-spot abbreviations, usually followed by needed elucidations, especially resemble more obscure present-day coinages like ANFAWFOS (and now for a word from our sponsor), TANSTAAFL (there ain't no such thing as a free lunch), ROFLEW (rolling on floor laughing while eating waffles), or the sesquipedalian RAOTFLMMFAOIATKFLMM (rolling around on the floor laughing my motherf——ing ass off in an attempt to keep from losing my mind).

But the Boston wits of 1838 and 1839 took abbreviation one step further toward both humor and obscurity by mangling the spelling. OK was not the first to be misspelled. In 1838, for example, Greene had used O.W. for *all right*, just as wrong as OK was when it made its appearance. (Another Boston publication used the correct abbreviation *a.r.* in February 1839, but that was evidently too tame for Greene and the *Morning Post*.)

By mid-1839 the fad for misspellings as well as abbreviations had hit New York too, evoking this comment in the *New York Evening Tattler* for July 27:

THE INITIAL LANGUAGE.—This is a species of spoken short-hand, which is getting into very general use among loafers and gentlemen of the fancy, besides Editors, to whom it saves, by its comprehensive expressiveness, much trouble in writing and many "ems" in printing. The Boston Morning Post made great use of it at one period. It is known that the City of the Pilgrims is an extremely aristocratic place, and that "our first men" are referred to constantly. Charley Green of the Post always wrote O.F.M. Walter of the Boston Transcript, we believe, used to designate the Young Men's Society for the Amelioration of the Condition of the Indians—Y.M.S.A.C.I. We heard yesterday of a lady who said to a gentleman, who was about to take leave of her, "O.K.K.B.W.P." The gallant thought an instant and obligingly granted the fair one's request. What could she have meant but "One Kind Kiss Before We Part?"

It will be observed that in the above, those initials are used which, in the vulgar spelling, begin the words they are intended to signify. But this language is more original, richer and less comprehensible, when those initials are given which might possibly, some how or other, be employed by people who spell "on their own hook." For instance, "K.G." (no go), K.Y. (no use) and K.K.K. (commit no nuisance). The last would be highly useful at this time to those housekeepers who throw filth into the streets. Apropos to this is the toast given by a country schoolmaster. "The Three Rs—Reading, 'Riting and 'Rithmetic."

Internet communications nowadays do employ deliberate mis-spellings, but generally of whole words rather than initials: phishing (e-mail hoax fishing for personal and financial information), pwnd (owned, to be dominated), pron (porn), teh (misspelling of *the*; emphasizes next word). These have in common with OK the implication of insider knowledge, that those who use it deliberately share an understanding that others don't. In the case of OK, it's knowledge of the spelling of *all correct*.

Back in Boston in the late 1830s, the misspelling OW for *all right* was especially important in paving the way for a smooth launch and reception of OK. It's not just that they both begin with *A* misspelled as *O*. They also have practically the same meaning. To this day, dictionaries generally give the definition as well as the chief synonym for OK as "all right."

And *all right* itself was apparently an interesting newcomer in the 1830s. The earliest example of *all right* provided by the *Oxford English Dictionary* is from Charles Dickens's *Pickwick Papers* of 1837: "'Stand firm, Sam,' said Mr. Pickwick, looking down. 'All right, sir,' replied Mr. Weller."

1840

OLD KINDERHOOK
IS OK

IN 1839, ITS FIRST YEAR, OK WAS NOTHING MORE THAN A joke. It was just one among many clever and not-so-clever abbreviations passed around by newspaper editors aiming to be funny. And as the next year began, there was nothing to suggest that OK was destined for greatness. Just the opposite; OK was poised to die out in obscurity, like OFM (our first men), SP (small potatoes), GC (gin cocktail), and OK's fellow in misspelling, OW (all right), whenever the joke would get stale and bored editors would be ready to try other amusements.

For OK, then, the year 1840 began uneventfully, with just a jokey OK here and a jokey OK there. But then a funny thing happened: a presidential election. Thanks to the accident of an election with unparalleled popular participation, OK was drafted to serve in the campaign of 1840. And though the OK candidate lost, by the end of the year OK itself was a winner, indelibly impressed in the American psyche across the length and breadth of the Republic. Or perhaps more accurately, just running amok.

For OK wasn't content to abide by a single meaning in 1840. Once the idea had been planted that OK could mean something in addition to "all correct," politicians, editors, and would-be poets outdid each other in conjuring fanciful new meanings for the two letters. Where OK had been in danger of fading into obscurity at the start of 1840, by year's end it was in danger of dissipating from meaning too many things to too many people. As luck would have it, it was saved from the latter fate only by a hoax about its origin—also involved with the election, and also in 1840.

Never before or since that year of 1840 has OK seen such radical change. Evolution, as Charles Darwin was to describe the process two decades later, is a good way to understand the development of OK in that memorable year. The bizarre politicking and editorializing of 1840 created an unusual temporary environment in which the fittest abbreviation to survive was none other than OK.

Old Kinderhook

The campaign of 1840 was a spectacular one, famous for its rallies, slogans, and symbols, in which OK played a prominent part.

The stage was set for OK in 1840 because it happened that Martin Van Buren was president of the United States and seeking a second term. And it happened that his home, where he was born and where he lived while not in Washington, was the upstate New York town of Kinderhook. Earlier in his political career Van Buren was known as the "Little Wizard" or "Little Magician" for his skill in building political coalitions (and for his short stature; he was five foot six). Now, noticing *K* in the name of his hometown, and noticing that Van Buren was advanced enough in age no longer to be called a young man (he was fifty-seven in 1840), someone in the Democratic Tammany political organization of New York City put that *K* together with the previous year's OK, calling Van Buren "Old Kinderhook." That nickname picked up the 1839 abbreviation like a magnet. OK now could have a double meaning: Old Kinderhook was all correct.

And Van Buren needed the power of OK, because he faced an opponent with some of the most effective campaign slogans of all time. The Whig candidate, old William Henry Harrison, campaigned on "Tippecanoe and Tyler Too," Tippecanoe reminding voters of General Harrison's victory over Indians at Indiana's Tippecanoe River in 1811, and John Tyler being Harrison's vice presidential candidate. But even more effective was the Harrison slogan "Log Cabin and Hard Cider." Strangely enough, it came from a derisive invention by an anti-Harrison journalist, John de Ziska, in the *Baltimore Republican* of December 11, 1839:

> Give him [Harrison] a barrel of hard cider, and settle a pension of two thousand a year on him, and my word for it, he will sit the remainder of his days in his log cabin by the side of a "sea coal" fire, and study moral philosophy.

After other Democrats picked up on this and repeated the intended insult, the Whigs decided to turn it around and make the most of it, portraying Harrison as a man of the people, supposedly living in a log cabin in Indiana with a barrel of hard cider outside. Harrison, in fact, lived in a grand Indiana mansion, but ever since the election of Andrew Jackson, Van Buren's predecessor as president, an association with a log cabin was highly useful in demonstrating that a candidate was a man of the people. So popular

was the image of "Log Cabin and Hard Cider" that it even was
depicted on elegant tea sets.

The Tammany OK

The rough and ready Tammany Society of New York City was at
the center of Democratic politicking, having supported Jackson
for his two terms as well as the election in 1836 of Jackson's hand-
picked successor, Van Buren. On March 23, 1840, exactly a year
after the birth of OK, a Tammany newspaper, the *New Era*, carried
this announcement:

> THE DEMOCRATIC O.K. CLUB, are hereby ordered to meet
> at the House of Jacob Colvin, 245 Grand Street, on Tuesday
> evening, 24th inst. at 7 o'clock.
>
> Punctual attendance is requested.
>
> By order,
>
> WILLIAM STOKELY, President
>
> John H. Low, Secretary

And what happened at that meeting? We can guess what they
talked about from what came next. Like the other Tammany clubs
in New York City—the Butt Enders, the Huge Paws, the Locofocos,
the Simon Pures, the Tammany Temple, and oh yes, the Van Buren
Association—the O.K. Club literally fought its Whig enemies.
On March 27, the *New Era* used OK to tell its Tammany readers
about a Whig meeting they ought to attend:

MEETING TO NIGHT O. K.

> The British Whig papers of this city contain a call for a public
> meeting to be held *this evening* in Masonic hall. . . . Those
> "who would render the right of universal suffrage easy of exercise

and convenient to all" are requested according to the call to be in attendance. To all such we say go.

And to that meeting they went, the O.K. Club in particular. According to the Newark *Daily Advertiser,* one of the many newspapers that next day reported the encounter:

> The doors being closed, some 15 or 20 Whigs remained in conversation, when some 60 rowdies burst suddenly in upon them with personal violence—both parties tearing away banisters and benches for weapons. A posse of watchmen soon rushed in and arrested the ringleaders. The *war cry* of the locofocos was O.K., the two letters paraded at the head of an inflammatory article in the New Era of the morning. "Down with the whigs, boys, O.K." was the shout of these poor, deluded men. Such were the fearful beginnings of the French Revolution!

Not to be outdone, the Whigs responded with a twist on O.K. The *Daily Express* commented a few days later,

> "O.K."—Many are puzzled to know the definition of these mysterious letters. It is Arabic, reads backwards, and means *kicked out*—of Masonic Hall. *Vide* Loco Foco Dictionary.

In turn, the Democratic *New Era* quickly picked up on K.O.:

> K.O.—O.K.—The Ohio City Transcript (federal) is K.O. (kicked over) and defunct—which is held to be O.K. (oll korrect).

O.K. figured in a Democratic parade on April 10. According to the *New Era* the next day, marchers carried a banner showing

> a huge Cabbage mounted upon legs, singing out O.K. to General Harrison, and chasing him like a racer.

At that point, the Tammany adoption of O.K. was something of a mystery. Why would a political club adopt a misspelled abbreviation for "all correct" as its war cry? On May 27 the *New Era* provided the explanation:

> JACKSON BREAST PIN.—We acknowledge the receipt of a very pretty gold Pin, representing the "old white hat with a crape" such as is worn by the hero of New Orleans, and having upon it the (to the "Whigs") very frightful letters O.K., significant of the birthplace of Martin Van Buren, old Kinderhook, as also the rallying word of the Democracy of the late election, "all correct." It can be purchased at Mr. P. L. Fierty's, 486 Pearl Street. Those who wear them should bear in mind that it will require their most strenuous exertions between this and autumn, to make all things O.K.

Oll Krazy for OK

Though the Democrats tried to keep O.K. for themselves, the Whigs made use of it too, sometimes in reporting election successes (as in "Cleveland O.K.!!"), sometimes in mockingly reinterpreting the initials, as in this from the Whig *Daily Express*:

> O.K., i.e. "Ole Korrect," Out of "Kash," Out of "Kredit," Out of "Karacter," and Out of "Klothes."

It wasn't just in New York either, though New York's Tammany is where the political OK began. But the campaign brought OK far afield from the eastern cities. A history of Ohio tells of a memorable day in Champaign County of west-central Ohio, population 16,720 in 1840:

Urbana was early somewhat famed for its political conventions. The largest probably ever held in the county was September 15, 1840, in the Harrison campaign, when an immense multitude assembled from counties all around. A cavalcade miles in extent met General Harrison and escorted him from the west to the Public Square, where he was introduced to the people by Moses B. Corwin and made a speech two hours in length. He was at this time sixty-seven years of age, but his delivery was clear and distinct. Dinner was had in the grove of Mr. John A. Ward, father of the sculptor, in the southwest part of the town, where twelve tables, each over 300 feet long, had been erected and laden with provisions. Oxen and sheep were barbecued, and an abundance of cider supplied the drink for the day. In the evening addresses were made by Arthur Elliott, ex-Governor Metcalf, of Kentucky, who wore a buckskin hunting shirt, Mr. Chambers, from Louisiana, and Richard Douglass, of Chillicothe. The day was one of great hilarity and excitement. The delegations and processions had every conceivable mode of conveyance and carried flags and emblems with various strange mottoes and devices. Among them was a banner or board, on which was this sentence:

> ## THE PEOPLE IS OLL KORRECT.

(The box is in the original.) And the 1891 history book concludes: "This was the origin of the use of the letters 'O. K.,' not uncommon in our own time." It wasn't the origin, but the denizens of Champaign County may be pardoned for not perusing the Boston newspapers of 1839.

Meanwhile, in Columbus, Ohio, the *Straight-out Harrisonian* offered this distinction in its issue of October 9, 1840:

> The Whig definition of O.K. is—Oll Koming. Locofoco [Democratic] definition—Orful Katastrophe.

With pundits and politicians gleefully appropriating OK for their peculiar purposes, it began to spin out of control. The *Oxford English Dictionary* quotes the *Lexington Intelligencer* of October 9:

> O.K. Perhaps no two letters have ever been made the initials of as many words as O.K. . . . When first used they were said to mean Out of Kash, (cash); more recently they have been made to stand for Oll Korrect, Oll Koming, Oll Konfirmed, &c. &c.

Exemplifying the *Intelligencer*'s claim, the Democratic *New Era* was happy to join in the imaginative interpretations of OK. On the eve of the election, the *New Era* printed a letter proposing nearly a dozen politically charged versions:

> Mr. Editor—Everything that we see, hear, or discourse of, is O.K., any *thing* otherwise is out of my power to imagine, and from *mature consideration,* I have arrived at the following conclusions:
>
> That Harrison, being the friend and advocate of Hard Cider, which (no doubt he freely uses) is O.K. "Olways Korned."
>
> That the "immortal Dan" [Webster] being Harrison's adviser in all political matters, is O.K. because he is Harrison's "own Konfidential."
>
> That "Henry [Clay] of the West" is likewise O.K. derived from no other source but his name "Old Klay."
>
> That MARTIN VAN BUREN, is O.K. because what he says is OLWAYS CREDITED, and what he does is OLL KORRECT.
>
> . . .

That General Jackson is O.K. because he is "Olways Kandid."

. . .

That the whigs engaged in committing the frauds on the Ballot Box in the fall of '33, and spring of '34, are O.K. because they are "Orful Konspirators."

That Moses H. Grinnell, the president candidate for Congress, is O.K. because he is at present "Orfully Konfused."

. . .

That my article is O.K. because it is OLL COMPOSED.

When the election of 1840 was over and Old Kinderhook had lost, Charles Gordon Greene of the *Boston Morning Post,* the daddy of OK, offered some ruefully humorous new interpretations for OK. In the issue of November 28:

O.K.—After the 4th of March next [with the inauguration of Whig President William Henry Harrison], these expressive initials will signify *all kwarrelling.* The whig house, divided against itself, cannot stand.

And on December 7:

Why shall we be O.K. after the first of January next? Because we shall be an *Ousted Kernel* [Greene himself was known as Colonel Greene].

Happy 1840, OK!

An exuberant writer, known only as C.B., summed up the situation of OK a year and a half after its birth in a poem that was published in the *Boston Daily Times* on December 15, 1840, and rediscovered by researcher Richard Walser in the 1960s. The poem refers to the presidential election where editor Greene was on the

THE LOG CA[BIN]

NEW JERSEY.

OFFICIAL.

	HARRISON.	VAN BUREN.
Atlantic	425	846
Bergen	977	1349
Burlington	3417	2405
Cape May	696	494
Cumberland	1497	1190
Essex	4636	2832
Gloucester	2288	1773
Hudson	726	501
Hunterdon	1850	2783
Mercer	2022	1494
Middlesex	2014	1683
Monmouth	2953	2830
Morris	2309	2150
Passaic	1362	962
Salem	1582	1362
Somerset	1721	1345
Sussex	1171	2322
Warren	1419	2466
	33,351	31,034
	31,034	

Harrison's maj. 2,317

The exact vote of each candidate for Elector was

Condict	33,340	Depue	31,032
Lupton	33,350	Fairchild	31,034
Iliff	33,358	Cassedy	31,051
Ryerson	33,352	Bigelow	31,033
Runk	33,350	Van Deursen	31,029
Wright	33,349	Sloan	31,032
Newbold	33,362	Hulme	30,578
Townsend	33,346	Stull	31,015

The difference between the two highest, Newbold and Fairchild, is 3328.

Mr. Hulme, (L. F.) received 449 votes in Gloucester in a wrong name, which should be added to his vote.

The Abolition ticket received 25 in Essex, 2 in Gloucester, 6 in Hudson, 2 in Monmouth, 13 in Morris, 18 in Passaic, 1 in Salem and 2 in Sussex. Total 69.

One ticket in Sussex for the Whig electors, containing only their last names, was not counted for them.

Presidential Election.

COMPLETE.

	HARRISON.	VAN BUREN.
MAINE,	10	
NEW HAMPSHIRE,		7
VERMONT	7	
MASSACHUSETTS	14	
RHODE ISLAND,	4	
CONNECTICUT,	8	
NEW YORK,	42	
NEW JERSEY,	8	
PENNSYLVANIA,	30	
DELAWARE	3	
MARYLAND	10	
VIRGINIA		23
NORTH CAROLINA,	15	
SOUTH CAROLINA,		11
GEORGIA,	11	
ARKANSAS		3
LOUISIANA	5	
OHIO,	21	
KENTUCKY,	15	
INDIANA,	9	
TENNESSEE,	15	
MISSISSIPPI,	4	
MICHIGAN,	3	
MISSOURI,		4
ILLINOIS		5
ALABAMA		7
	234	60

Whole number of Electoral votes, 294—Necessary to a choice, 148 votes.

The Popular Voice.

The following table exhibits the popular vote, in the several States, as far as the official returns have been received:

	HARRISON.	VAN BUREN.

NEW-HAMPSHIRE.

COMPLETE.

	Pres't, Nov. 1840.		Gov. March, 1840
	Har.	V. B.	(W.) (L. F.)
Rockingham	4942	7559	3100 8246
Strafford	5362	6755	4179 6001
Merrimack	4790	5026	2105 4440

The *Log Cabin Advocate* of December 15, 1840
Triumphant Pro-Harrison Newspaper Reporting Election Results

losing side, and to much else. There is no better way to show how widely by then OK had spread its fame and its meanings than to reprint it here in full. The particular political posturings matter less for our purpose than the inventive uses for OK.

O.K.

What is't that ails the people, Joe?
They're in a kurious way,
For every where I chance to go,
There's nothing but o.k.
They do not use the alphabet,
What e'er they wish to say,
And all the letters they forget,
Except the o. and k.

I've seen them on the Atlas' page,
And also in the Post,
When both were boiling o'er with rage,
To see which fibbed the most.
The *Major* [editor of the *Atlas*] has kome off the best;
The *Kernel* [editor Greene] is surprised!
The one it seems meant *oll korrect*,
The other, *oll kapsized!*

Processions have been all the go,
And illuminations tall;
Hand bills were headed with k. o.,
Which means, they say, *kome oll!*
The way the people sallied out,
Was a kaution to the lazy;
And when o. k. I heard them shout,
I thought it meant *oll krazy*.

They say that *Blair*, the editor,
Is o. k. off to Kuba,
But what it is he's gone there for,
Is nothing but false rumor.
K. k., the konkered kandidate,
Must yield to freedom's right;
He's a handsome man, but k. k. k.,
He *kould not kome it kwite!*

There's *Butler* too, in whom, Whigs say,
No man kan safely trust;
They tell him oft to k. k. k.,
Keep karefully his krust.
The people thought when he took hold
To prove that votes were bought,
A monstrous fraud would kwick be told,
With Whigs, o. k., *oll kaught!*

The Merchants too have been o. k.,
Hard times have loudly said it;
It long has been too much their way,
To buy and sell *on kredit.*
They'll now adopt as bad a kourse,
Be o. k., *over cautious*,
Which constantly will prove a source
Of miseries and tortures.

The President, that big steam ship,
Has acted very droll;
She was o. k. her second trip,
For she got *out of koal.*
K. k. k. is the proper name

For all the New York boats;
Kunard kan konquer on the main
Each steamer that it floats.

The would be swell, whose purse is drained,
Who *kannot kut* a dash:
To see o. k., his heart is pained,
Bekause he's *out of kash;*
He e'en resolved to kut his throat,
But feels somewhat afraid,
He views o. k., his *orful koat,*
And *Earle's last* bill unpaid.

Whene'er you read an accident,
'Tis o. k. that you see;
An *orrible kalamity,*—
Orful katastrophe.
And when the people rave and rant
About some trifling thing,
You'll find it's all o. k., *oll kant,*
Which makes the *kountry* ring.

They're running k. k.'s in the street,
And handsomely they go;
I've heard them kalled *konvenient Kabs,*
By one who ought to know:—
He said he rode in one, one day,
When heavily it stormed,
And thought them just the thing for those
Who are o. k., *oll korned* [drunk].

The beauteous girls, unkonsciously,
Kause many sad regrets,

They love so well to be o. k.,
Such *orrible kokettes!*
I know of one whose flaxen hair,
Hangs down o. k., *oll kurly;*
Her lips the sweets of Eden bear,
And more,—she ne'er speaks surly.

To win this angel's heart and hand,
I used o. k., *oll kunning;*
And thought to make my konverse grand,
By great attempts at punning.
'Twas all in vain,—she merely said
She liked me as a friend,
And now she's gulling a young blade,
Whose love thus sad will end.

The *kry of* o. k. rends the air,
From north to south it goes,—
It's on a shop in Brattle Square,
Where negroes sell *old klothes!*
The world ne'er saw such kurious times,
Since politics were born,—
You'll see o. k. on grain-store signs,
Which stands for *Oats and Korn!*

This theme has on Pegasus' way
Most wantonly obtruded,
And now, with joy, I have to say
It's o. k. *oll konkluded.*
Yet four more lines I needs must write,
From which there's no retreat,
O. k. again I must endite,
And—lo! it's *oll komplete!*

Three days later, referring to a reprint of the poem in a weekly newspaper, the *Times* commented: "O.K. our readers will certainly admit is o.k." Clearly, the core meaning of OK remained intact, but it was threatening to expand its periphery to encompass a large chunk of the language.

Against Expectations

By its very nature, OK had already violated the first rule for survival of a vocabulary creation: blend in, be inconspicuous. Conspicuous coinages can't compete. Clever comments aren't incorporated. Jokes don't blend into the common vocabulary.

The evidence for this principle is overwhelming (and given at length in my 2002 book *Predicting New Words: The Secrets of Their Success*). For just one example: In the 1980s Rich Hall published five books of *sniglets,* "words that don't appear in the dictionary but should," such as *mustgo,* "any item of food that has been sitting in the refrigerator so long it has become a science project." Of all his invented words, the only one that ever caught on was *sniglets* itself. The others were too clever, too conspicuous.

And OK was conspicuous. It kalled attention to itself by its misspelling, by its use of the konspikuous *K* (katching, isn't it?), and by its origin as a joke, which in turn inspired other jokes. Indeed, OK called ekstreme attention to itself. It's hard to imagine any other koinage of American English evoking a 112-line poem.

End of the Road?

Paradoxically, as 1840 drew to a close, the very prominence of OK put it in danger of demise. With so conspicuous an appearance, and such possibilities for dispersion of meaning, OK was on the verge of vanishing into thin air, leaving behind only its smile, a chuckle to be known only to historians of early nineteenth-century American politics. Instead, it was saved by yet another joke, the subject of the next chapter.

4

HOAX

ANDREW JACKSON'S
MISSPELLING

THANKS TO JOKESTERS AND POLITICIANS, OK WAS RIDING HIGH
a year after its birth. But its rise was in danger of being meteoric,
a mere flash in the pan, because konspikuous klever koinages
rarely make it into the everyday vocabulary of a language. We
laugh at them or with them, we play with them, and then we set
them aside when we return to everyday discourse.

Indeed, having gone through the wringer in the election of
1840, OK was too conspicuous, too much of a joke, and too mul-
tifarious in its range of meanings to slip under the tent of the
permanent general vocabulary. By the end of that year it had
sprouted so many joking meanings that it was on the verge of
evaporating into meaninglessness. A miracle would be needed
to save it from being a mere footnote to the history of Boston

newspaperdom or early nineteenth-century American politics. But a miracle did appear, and in a most unlikely form.

No, the miracle wasn't a sober essay on the practical uses of OK. Nor was it a plea for open-mindedness and respect for others, expressed as "I'm OK, you're OK"; that interpretation wouldn't be invented until well over a century later. Instead, it was a political hoax, meant as a satirical joke but taken seriously by both sides in that 1840 presidential election. Once the hoax was successfully launched, the place of OK in our language was secure.

Andrew Jackson's Orthography

To understand the OK hoax of 1840, it is necessary to go back more than a decade to the election of 1828, which brought Andrew Jackson, Martin Van Buren's Democratic predecessor, to the White House. Jackson's immense popularity in turn propelled Van Buren into his own first presidency, in 1836, and Van Buren was still being extolled as Old Hickory's candidate in the 1840 election. During that election an opponent of Van Buren wrote a bogus story mocking Jackson that eventually made OK a household word.

Jackson was known for his humble origins, in pointed contrast to the aristocratic background of his six predecessors as president of the United States. Jackson's partisans in the elections of 1824 (when he lost to aristocratic John Quincy Adams), 1828 (when he won), and 1832 (when he won again) turned previous presidential qualifications on their head and boasted that he was a man of the common people. Why, Jackson was even born in a log cabin.

Indeed, the log cabin became such a potent political symbol that for the rest of the nineteenth century presidential candidates associated themselves with log cabins if they could. Notable in the case of the election of 1840, which did so much for OK, was the reinvention of aristocratic William Henry Harrison as a man of "log cabin and hard cider."

But getting back to Jackson: While a majority of his fellow citizens admired his rise from humble beginnings, others questioned whether a person so apparently lacking in education should be allowed to hold the office of president.

In fact, Jackson's education was not as lacking as might appear. He attended school for several years, his mother intending him for the ministry. That didn't work; she died when he was fourteen, and his temperament and hot temper were manifestly unsuited to a clerical career. Nevertheless, he was educated enough to spend two years as a schoolteacher, followed by three years reading law with two eminent lawyers, the usual way of preparing for a legal career before the days of law schools. He obtained his law license in 1787, at age twenty, and went on to be a district attorney, a county judge, and a judge of the Tennessee Superior Court. By the time he was elected president in 1828, he had also served as a U.S. senator. He was skilled in the use of language.

Nevertheless, his opponents assumed that anyone with so poor a background (and perhaps also with such a rough temperament) must be illiterate—or at least a bad speller. And so in Jackson's successful presidential campaign of 1828, as documented by Allen Walker Read, his ability to spell was impugned first by one hostile newspaper and then another, often in satire and sarcasm.

The first attack came in a Washington newspaper in February 1828. It was a hoax, though not the one that later would give OK new life. The paper printed this letter, purportedly from Jackson himself:

To the Editors of the Washington Journal.

When the midnight assasins plunges his dagger to the heart &
riffles your goods, the turpitude of this scene looses all its horrors
when compared with the act of the secrete assasins poniard
leveled against femal character by the hired minions of power.

If you could believe its authenticity—and probably only the
blindest anti-Jacksonians actually did—it was a shocking revelation
of the cacography, not to mention lunacy, of Andrew Jackson.

The battle was joined. Misspellings are a tempting topic for
print publications, offering easy targets for denunciation and ridi-
cule, so both sides in the 1828 election embraced the opportunity.
Other newspapers joined in, reprinting the *Journal* letter and arguing, for example, in this blast from the *New York American*: "Now,
we think it rather hard that in a country whose proud and just boast
it is that common school education is more universally diffused
than in any other, the candidate for chief magistracy should be defi-
cient even in the elements of orthography and grammar."

Jackson's partisans dismissed the *Washington Journal* letter as
fake, especially after a pro-Jackson delegation visited the editor of
the *Journal* and asked him to produce the original. He couldn't.
All he could show them was a printed pamphlet purportedly
reproducing the handwriting of the letter. According to the pro-
Jackson *United States Telegraph* of the capital city:

The Editor of [the *Journal*], Mr. Force, was then told by those
gentlemen that they did not believe the manuscript was the
hand writing of General Jackson; and one of them added, he
thought he could conveniently find a dozen persons, at least,
who could imitate Gen. Jackson's hand writing equally as well
as the person who had attempted an imitation of it. . . .

Hundreds of persons in society, have sufficient materials, from which, to refute such a pitiful and contemptible slander: but these disciples of the professor of rhetoric [John Quincy Adams, Jackson's opponent], are almost deranged from a fear that the people are about to furnish themselves with a President, who sprung from a common family, who has not been educated at Foreign Courts.

The argument continued throughout that election year of 1828, with each side presenting letters more or less authentic in support of their view of Jackson's orthography. For example, a Jackson partisan wrote in the *New York Enquirer*:

To say that the hero of New-Orleans, the Governor of a Territory, a Judge in his own State, a man who has enjoyed the confidence of every republican administration in this country—to say that such a man cannot spell the commonest word, and to say it seriously too, is too much for poor human nature to bear.

Meanwhile, a doggerel poet for an anti-Jackson newspaper, the *New Jersey Eagle*, didn't worry about authentic documents but invented these lines, as if in Jackson's own words:

Then a nice *writing-man* I have hired for my use,
To hide the bad *spelin* I *skrawl*—
And *them are* as *says* how my grammar is bad,
Don't know nothing of it at all.

Jackson's supposed inability to spell did not turn away every voter. A Jacksonian editor, writing for the *New York Enquirer*, told of a farmer who, having been lectured by an "exact orthographer" who "gave a long dissertation in favor of Adams," commented, "I never found a dictionary man that was not half a fool—I'm for Hickory, I believe."

One more aspect of Andrew Jackson's spelling ability, or lack of it, would turn out to be important for the development of OK more than a decade later: his misspellings were said to include *K* where *C* should be. A writer for the pro-Jackson *United States Telegraph*, also in 1828, claimed that Adams's partisans were looking through Jackson letters in the War Office to find evidence of misspelling, and sarcastically added:

> We are positively assured the following will appear: that he spells C-oalition with a K; Hartford C-onvention after the same manner; likewise C-ongress; fails to dot his *eyes* and cross his *teas*; and withal is so wholly unacquainted with the simple words, bargain, intrigue and management, as not to be able to spell them at all.

Nearly two centuries later, we can look more dispassionately at the evidence, which shows Jackson to be neither a terrible speller nor a perfect one. Here, for example, is the first paragraph of a private letter he wrote to his wife while negotiating an Indian treaty in Mississippi:

CHIKESAW COUNCIL HOUSE SEPT. 18TH. 1816

MY LOVE,

I have this moment recd. your affectionate letter of the 8th. Instant, I rejoice that you are well & our little son. Tell him his sweet papa hears with pleasure that he has been a good boy & learns his Book, Tell him his sweet papa labours hard to get money to educate him, but when he learns & becomes a great man, his sweet papa will be amply rewarded for all his care, expence, & pains—how thankfull I am to you for taking poor little Lyncoya home & cloathing him—I have been much hurt to see him there with the negroes, like a lost sheep without a sheperd.

But whether or not Jackson was a good speller is beside the point as far as OK is concerned. What matters is that the story of his cacography, including the substitution of *K* for *C*, was widespread, making possible, more than a decade later, the hoax that would make OK a permanent addition to our language.

Just as we know the name of the creator of OK in Boston in 1839, so we have the good fortune to know who perpetrated the OK hoax in 1840. It was James Gordon Bennett, a man whose political position had changed between 1828 and 1840. In 1828, Bennett was the Washington correspondent for the pro-Jackson *New York Enquirer*. For the April 24, 1828, issue of the *Enquirer* he sent this dispatch, defending Jackson by the novel ploy of revealing the bad spelling habits of other notables. This is how he supported Jackson against those who were aghast at the general's misspellings:

> You have doubtless read whole columns in the coalition papers attempting to show that General Jackson cannot spell, read, or write. I was amusing myself the other day in the Library of Congress, where the fine ladies and gentlemen congregate to talk politics, literature, fashion and dress, and, by chance, came to examine those *fac-similes* of several hand writings of men of renown, which are generally inserted in their biographies.
>
> Who would dare to say that Edmund Burke could not spell? Yet, I can prove it "by construction," and following literally the exact form of his letters. In Prior's Life of Burke, published in 1824, there are two *fac-simile* receipts in Burke's autograph to Dodsley, in which, there are five words in forty misspelled—such as *rejestir,* for register, *biy,* for being, *annial,* for annual, &c. In Pope's autograph of the translation of the Iliad, contained in D'Israeli's Curiosities of Literature, several of his words could be "construed" into errors—such as *illustrous* for illustrious, *bey* for

boy, *Hecter* for Hector, *gental* for gentle, and *o thou* at the beginning of a line of poetry. In an autograph frank of Joseph Addison, when Secretary of State, there is a mistake in his capital letters.

I could enumerate many other instances of a like nature; but these will be, in part, sufficient, to expose the folly of attempting to show, that eminent men cannot spell, provided their words are fastidiously examined. I could prove in the same way that Canova, the celebrated Italian artist, and Sir Christopher Wren, the great English architect, could not spell their own names. Look at Napoleon's handwriting, and it would appear that he could not spell a single word. . . .

One of the most curious instances of bad spelling is contained in the Life of Elbridge Gerry, by James T. Austin, a work just published in Boston. In this volume there is a *fac-simile* of Gerry's handwriting, in which carried is spelled *carred*, colonies spelled as *colenies*, besides several other words which could very easily be construed into blunders. The most curious is a mistake in Gerry's own Christian name; for by an examination it will be found that he spells Elbridge by substituting an l for a b—thus, *Ellridge*. I have recently seen several manuscripts of other great men of this country. Jefferson begins no other sentence with a capital letter but the first word of a paragraph.

This is also somewhat the practice of General Jackson, whose handwriting is rapid and flowing, and it has been imputed to him as a species of ignorance.

The Legend of "Ole Kurrek"

On and on Bennett's report continues with other examples showing that Jackson, if he misspelled, did so in good company. But now jump a dozen years ahead to the election of 1840. This time James Gordon Bennett was editor of the *New York Morning Herald*, a highly successful penny newspaper he had founded in 1835. Instead of supporting Jackson's Democratic successor Martin Van Buren for reelection, Bennett took Harrison's side. But it doesn't really matter whose side he was on. What matters is that just three days after OK entered the political fray in a pro-Jackson newspaper as a rallying cry for Tammany supporters of the president, Bennett responded with this story in his newspaper:

> THE O. K. CLUB—O. K. LITERATURE.—This gang of loafers and litterateurs, who broke in upon the Whigs at Masonic Hall on Friday evening last, and kicked up the row there, are said to number 1000 bravos, being the picked men of the old "huge paws"—"butt enders"—"roarers," and "ball rollers." The origin of their name, O. K. is curious and characteristic. A few years ago, some person accused Amos Kendall [a pro-Jackson newspaper editor and later Jackson's postmaster general] to General Jackson, of being no better than he should be. "Let me examine the papers," said the old hero, "I'll soon tell whether Mr. Kendall is right or wrong." The General did so and found every thing right. "Tie up them papers," said the General. They were tied up. "Mark on them, "O. K.," continued the General. O. K. was marked upon them. "By the Eternal," said the good old General, taking his pipe from his mouth, "Amos is *Ole Kurrek* (all correct) and no mistake," blowing the smoke up the chimney's cheek. After this the character of Amos was established on the rock of Gibraltar. Harvard College, on hearing of this event, was thrown into extacies, and made the General an LL.D., which he is to this day.

The O. K.s are now the most original and learned locofoco club of the day. Their arguments are the most convincing test logicians ever invented.

Some of Bennett's allusions need explication for modern readers. "Locofocos" was a nickname for the Democrats, especially the Tammany version, and their partisans went by the nicknames Bennett uses in his first sentence: "huge paws" referred to workingmen and farmers, for example, and "ball rollers" to men who literally rolled giant balls in political parades, another practice introduced in the presidential campaign of 1840.

More relevant to OK is the reference to Harvard. In 1833, Harvard University awarded Jackson an honorary doctor of laws degree. This infuriated ex-president John Quincy Adams, the rhetorician, who was still bitter about losing the 1828 election to a supposed illiterate. He wrote to the president of Harvard asking that the degree not be awarded, only to get this reply: "As the people have twice decided that this man knows law enough to be their ruler, it is not for Harvard College to maintain that they are mistaken." Adams grumbled in his diary, "I would not be present to witness her [Harvard's] disgrace in conferring her highest literary honors upon a barbarian who could not write a sentence of grammar and could hardly spell his own name."

Learning of this, legend says, Jackson supposedly retorted, "It is a damn poor mind indeed which can't think of at least two ways to spell any word." But whether or not Jackson actually made that remark, the Harvard degree kept the accusation of Jackson's illiteracy before the public. It led easily to Bennett's 1840 embellishment of the legend by the addition of OK.

That this story of Bennett's was meant as a joke and not an actual historical account is confirmed by another spoofing item in the same vein, a purported letter to the editor in response to his article that Bennett published in his *Morning Herald* three days later:

O.K.

NEW YORK MAR 27TH 1840

MR BENETT

Sir—You have taken the leborty to Slander us most publickly in this mornings paper. the O.K. Institute which you hav so falsely represented was established for our own pleasure and enjoyment and was never intended for sich a d—d Rascale as your self

J A MEMBER
WHICH YOU WAS MEAN ENOUGH TO PURSENATE.

ANSWER.—I cry you mercy, O.K. I have no wish to depreciate from the high reputation of so erudite a Society. Nor shall I ever interfere with your amusements in knocking down people. Col. Webb and you may enjoy a monopoly of that business.—*Ed. Herald.*

This is further confirmation that Bennett, like Charles Gordon Greene when he invented OK a year earlier, was attempting humor rather than history.

However, it is easy to see why others would believe Bennett's tale of Jackson's "Ole Kurrek." It was the first attempt to explain the origin of OK, and it did so in a way that made sense. True or not, the claim that Jackson couldn't spell was well known; Bennett's story merely added another instance. Although he didn't give a date, he was quite particular about the occasion, as if he had exact historical knowledge. And after all, who would spell the initials of "all correct" as OK? Only a really bad speller, not the editor of a newspaper, for goodness' sake. And the best-known of all purported illiterates in America was Andrew Jackson. Q.E.D.

Furthermore, who wouldn't prefer a colorful story about a word's origin to a lame one?

In short, Bennett's is a much better story than the one about a Boston newspaper in 1839. It is amusing and logical. It just happens not to be true.

More than a century and a half since Bennett's story was printed, not a scrap of evidence has turned up to confirm it. There is no evidence of OK before Boston 1839 anywhere, whether in the papers of Andrew Jackson, the newspapers of the day, or anywhere else. Thanks to the extensive newspaper evidence unearthed by Allen Walker Read, we now know, beyond the shadow of a doubt, that OK sprang as a joke from the mind and pen of a Boston editor whose orthography was impeccable. But even in 1840, barely a year after the birth of OK, that explanation must have seemed less likely than the one attributing it to Andrew Jackson.

It was quickly adopted by other newspapers. By early April 1840, two newspapers in New York City and another in Albany had already picked up Bennett's story and offered it as a more or less authoritative explanation for OK, as in this report in the *New York Commercial Advertiser*:

> "O.K."—The meaning of these mysterious letters, the power of which, when exerted, is so fatal to the peace and harmony of the city, is a question of grave deliberation in certain quarters. We are not proficients in cabalistic puzzles; but it is asserted that these letters constituted the endorsement of General Jackson upon papers that he had examined and found right—thus, O.K.—*Oll Korrect.*

Two things about this report show the development from initial joke to established (though false) explanation. First, the mere existence of the report indicates that an explanation is needed. A simple parenthetical gloss of "all correct" for OK no longer would do, thanks to the Tammany appropriation of OK for political purposes. And as is often the case, a question about the meaning of a word has led to a desire to know its origin. Second, there is no indication that the author suspects the story to be anything but the truth. If Bennett's article had been taken as a joke, the writer likely would have been tempted to improve on it for humorous purposes, as we can surmise from the humorous exaggerations of "grave deliberation" and "cabalistic puzzles."

Major Jack Downing

By the summer of 1840, the story of the Jackson origin of OK had been enhanced by attribution to "Jack Downing," the pseudonym used by Seba Smith of Maine for humorous newspaper columns in a New England rustic dialect. "Downing," who was supposedly a confidant of President Jackson, indeed would have been a likely candidate to tell of Jackson's OK, whether as a true story or an invented anecdote. Someone likely said, "This must have come from Jack Downing," and before long that speculation became accepted as fact. This is how the *Boston Atlas* explained it in August 1840:

> O.K. These initials, according to Jack Downing, were first used by Gen. Jackson. "Those papers, Amos, are all correct. I have marked them O.K.," (oll korrect). The Gen. was never good at spelling.

The story is now a little different from Bennett's, as one might expect of an anecdote told and retold. Amos Kendall is now Jackson's interlocutor rather than the recipient of the OK mark, and Downing is the authority who vouches for the origin of OK. But the essential story has been firmly established.

The story of Jackson's OK made such sense that it was accepted, complete with attribution to the fictitious Major Jack Downing, in the authoritative book *Americanisms: The English of the New World* by Maximilian Schele de Vere, published in New York in 1872.

> American politics abound in catch-words, the great majority of which pass away with the accident that gave them birth, while others please the fancy of the populace, or acquire, by an unexpected success, such a hold on the public mind as to secure to them a longer lease of life. One of these is as ludicrous in its origin as tenacious in its persistency in the slang of the day. The story goes that General Jackson, better known in American history as *Old Hickory*, was not much at home in the art of spelling, and his friend and admirer, Major Jack Downing, found therefore no difficulty in convincing the readers of his "Letters," that the President employed the letters *O. K.* as an endorsement of applications for office, and other papers. They were intended to stand for "All Correct," which the old gentleman preferred writing *Oll Korrect*, and hence they are used, to this day, very much in the sense of the English "All Right." To the question how a convalescent is, the answer comes back: "Oh, he is quite O. K. again!"

As befits a careful scholar (an immigrant from Sweden, Schele de Vere was a professor of modern languages at the University of Virginia), Schele de Vere qualifies his account with "The story goes," but he tells it with gusto and offers no alternative.

Prompted by such stories, researchers have scoured the "Jack Downing" papers without finding any mention of OK. It's such a good story that, if true, Jack Downing surely would have told it. Evidently, however, OK is too outlandish to have been inadvertently invented by Old Hickory or anyone else. It could only have been invented as a joke, as it was, and then after the fact attributed to Jackson.

Enough of This Nonsense

OK. It remained for someone who actually knew how Jackson actually wrote to weigh in. This we find in an 1882 letter to the *St. Louis Globe-Democrat* by a man who had been a State Department clerk during Jackson's first term.

> To the Editor of the New York Sun.
>
> In your Saturday's issue "Jackson" says: "Gen. Jackson, when President, had certain papers laid before him, and marked them O.K., and when asked what it meant said, 'All correct.'" . . . From a very close and intimate connection with Gen. Andrew Jackson during his whole Presidency, from 1829 to 1838, I know that no such mode of indication inured to Gen. Jackson at all, and confident I am that he never could possibly have made use of such expressions. He was a very courteous and gentlemanly person, of much refinement and elegant expression. He retained his military habit of devolving all epistolary matters upon his Secretaries, and therefore left behind him very brief writings of any kind.

Someone who nowadays knows about Jackson's writing habits echoes this view. Thomas Coens, an associate editor of the present-day edition of Jackson's papers, states:

Jackson was orthographically challenged, but knew how to spell "correct," even on his worst days; and there's no evidence that he ever endorsed anything "all correct," however spelled. And Jackson never once, as far as I can tell, endorsed a document with an abbreviation—not with "A. C." or "O. K." or anything else.

It is quite possible, indeed likely, that Andrew Jackson went to his grave (he died in 1845) without ever uttering or writing OK. There is no record that he ever noticed the attribution of OK to him or responded to it.

Abraham and Zachary

Nevertheless, on the basis of that story, OK went to work. The Jackson hoax, even though it was laughable, put OK to serious use. At some point, Bennett's story, with its repetition and permutations by other hands, must have been the impetus and inspiration for the first person to imitate Jackson's supposed practice of marking papers with OK—for real. Perhaps it was a proofreader, or a scrivener like Herman Melville's Bartleby.

The practice must have been a little tongue in cheek at first, for anyone charged with approving a document would be enough of an orthographer to know that *O* and *K* were the wrong initials. Maybe he wrote OK in good humor. But perhaps he also noticed that the letters *O* and *K* make a more satisfying and distinctive mark than, say, *A* and *C*. *O* is a satisfying oval, all curves; *K* is all straight lines, a collection of sticks. The combination is stark and striking. OK was fortunate in its alphabetic heredity.

In contrast with the detailed evidence for OK as a joke and OK in politics in 1839 and 1840, there is a scarcity of information about the earliest actual users of the OK mark on documents. But in 1864, nearly a quarter century after the Jackson OK story saw print, there is a passing reference to the practice of marking OK on documents in an odd poem about Abraham Lincoln. It is yet another attempt at humor, so it needs to be taken with more than a grain of salt; and it purports to come from Liverpool, England, which distances it. But it is in an American magazine, *The Old Guard, A Monthly Journal; Dedicated to the Principles of 1776 and 1787*. Published in New York City from 1863 to 1867, *The Old Guard* was virulently proslavery, antiwar, and anti-Lincoln.

The poem, headed "Liverpool—September, 1864," is titled "Abraham's Vision—an Homeric Ode." The synopsis at the beginning explains: "In the following Ode, Abe is supposed to have fallen asleep after dinner. He dreamt he was shown the Future of his Country. The South had gained its Independence. Then, following on this, he sees the fate of his associates in government. Abe is spoken of as if he were really present."

Abe prays for a vision of the future, and Apollyon, a hellish visitor, obliges him with the postwar result: "Two countries with a President and flag for each." At that,

> Abraham, poor soul, was stricken dumb with fright,
> At the sad end of this his wished-for sight;
> His "lingual ribbon" once more moving free:
> "Guess, stranger, that view ain't O. K."† said he;
> "Reckon my country, sir, shall have a better fate;
> You'll see U-nited States again, I calculate."
> To whom Apollyon: "Sire, 'twas you express'd
> The wish to look; I see you're much distressed;
> If still you wish your *rulers'* fates to see,
> Then, summon courage, sire, and follow me."

And Lincoln is led to the underworld, to see the unhappy shades of Horace Greeley and the like. The dagger after O. K. links to a footnote that reads:

† O.K.—Anglice (Oil Kirrect,) all correct. First used by President Taylor in signing official documents during the Mexican War.

Humorous exaggeration is evident in the hyperelevated language of "lingual ribbon," the hyperlearned Latin "Anglice" for "in English," and the hypermisspelling of "Oil Kirrect," going beyond even the joking misspellings of 1839 and 1840. So we should not take for certain that Lincoln used OK or that President Zachary Taylor marked documents with OK. For that matter, Taylor wasn't president during the Mexican War; he wasn't elected until 1848, just after the war had come to a close. The "facts" of the poem indeed need to be taken with a grain of salt.

Yet there could be a germ of truth in the footnote to the poem. The Mexican War took place from 1846 to 1848, some years after the birth of OK and its attribution to Jackson, so it might have been in genuine use for documents then. And Taylor, then just General Taylor, was the most prominent military commander throughout the war, hero of the battles of Palo Alto in 1846 and of Buena Vista in 1847. Undoubtedly he had many occasions to send official reports back to President Polk in Washington. Though Taylor came from a prominent Virginia family, he had spent his childhood in a log cabin on the frontier and was known as "Old Rough and Ready," a man of the people in the Jacksonian mold. For what it's worth, he had a deserved reputation as a bad speller. Either in all seriousness or in conscious good humor, he may have marked OK on documents.

Old Jacob Astor

In 1881 a London author credited yet another American with the origin of the OK mark, none other than

> old Jacob Astor, the millionaire of New York. He was looked upon in commercial circles as a man of great information and sound judgment, and was a sort of general referee as to the solvency or standing of other traders. If a note of enquiry as to any particular trader's position came, the answer to which he intended to be satisfactory, he was accustomed to write across the note the letters "O.K.," and return it to the writer. The letters O.K. he supposed to be the initials of "all correct," and in this sense they are now universally current in the States.

Astor died in 1848, so it is possible that he, as well as Taylor, used O.K. in the 1840s. But whether or not they did, these stories are evidence that the practice of writing OK on documents was well known a few decades after its first telling. And the transposition from Jackson to Lincoln and Taylor and Astor shows that what made the greatest impression was not who supposedly did it but what they did.

The Professor's OK Mark

At last in 1871 there is confirming evidence that people were actually marking OK on documents to attest that they passed muster, and that this practice had been going on for some time. Strangely enough, it is yet another humorous item, but this time the joke is not about OK. It comes from academia, an item in the *Hamilton* [College] *Literary Monthly* for January 1871:

A Freshman at Cornell was recently horrified to find that he had handed his physiology notes to his professor in French, for examination and criticism. But what was his relief to receive his notes from said professor with the well known mark O.K., applied.

And so at the very latest by 1871, thirty years after it saw the light of day, OK had acquired its completely serious function as a mark of approval, all thanks to a joke.

Beyond a doubt, Bennett's story about Jackson's OK was a hoax. But also beyond a doubt, without that story, OK as we know it today would not exist. Indeed, chances are that OK would not exist at all except as a historical footnote. If Bennett had not published his article, the history of OK likely would have come to an inglorious end not long after the election of 1840.

AESTHETICS

THE LOOK AND
SOUND OF OK

IF A HUMOROUS ABBREVIATION MEANING "ALL RIGHT" WAS GOING
to enter our American vocabulary, why wouldn't it be OW? That
joke, the mock abbreviation for "oll wright," was already in circulation in the Boston press a year before OK came along. "All right"
was, and is, a more familiar expression than "all correct." So why did
OW fade and OK succeed?

As we have seen, it was partly a matter of politics. As luck
would have it, Martin Van Buren came from Kinderhook, New
York, not Watervliet. But the rise of OK was also helped by its
look and sound.

A circle with an asterisk. Smooth oval, cluster of sticks. Feminine
O, masculine *K*. That's the look of OK.

In print, on paper, or on the computer screen, in capital letters or lowercase, OK commands attention for joining extremes: of all the twenty-six letters of the alphabet, ultimate roundness and ultimate angularity.

That striking contrast gives it special effectiveness as a mark on papers or in headlines and is probably a reason why it was quickly put to use for both, even in the knowledge that OK was not the correct spelling for *all correct*. OW shows almost as much contrast, but *W* doesn't explode from its nucleus the way *K* does.

The correctly spelled abbreviation for OK also fares worse. AC does have angularity next to roundness, but the angles are more diffuse and the roundness is less complete. And while OK retains its contrast in lowercase ok, the *A* becomes curvy in lowercase, and the contrast round-angular is completely lost.

No other combination of letters, capital or lowercase, shows the contrast of OK. Even the same letters when reversed show less contrast, because the *K* in OK looks away from *O*; in KO it looks toward it.

Surely the look of the OK combination was not in Charles Gordon Greene's mind when he launched OK (as o. k.) on March 23, 1839. But just as surely, that striking combination was an attraction, even if subconscious, for the politicians who picked up OK in 1840 and the scribes who (perhaps jokingly at first) began writing OK on documents, supposedly in imitation of Andrew Jackson.

Its striking look was also emphasized because of *K*, the most striking letter of the English alphabet. *K* is pekuliar bekause it kan be substituted for *C* and still konvey with klarity the meaning and pronunciation of a word. In fact, it is less ambiguous in pronunciation than the *C* it replaces.

For a long time, *K* was a rarity in the English alphabet, the *K* sound largely represented by the letter *C*. But when *I* and *E* after

C made the *C* sound like *S*, as in *cinder* and *certain*, *K* gradually came to be used to make clear that *king* and *keep* were pronounced with the *K* sound. There aren't too many such words, amounting to only a dozen pages of a thousand-page dictionary. So in English, *K* remains scarce.

Put a *K* where it is not needed, therefore, and it klowns around, katching attention but not kausing konfusion. Real-life examples of this are plentiful. Indeed, there was a "kraze for *K*" around the time of OK's birth, manifested in attempts at humor like this one from a Chicago newspaper in April 1839:

> The Eight K's. The Hon. Henry Clay was denominated the Eight K's, by a coterie of wags in Washington, during the last session of Congress. He acquired this title thus: a gentleman sitting in the gallery of the Senate chamber during an interesting debate, wished to point out Mr. Clay to his friend, a foreigner, who sat beside him, without disturbing the house, and wrote upon a card for him, thus:—"The gentleman to the left of the speaker, in klaret kolored koat with krimson kollar, is Mr. Klay, member of Kongress from Kentucky."

Kodak is a famous example of a nineteenth-century company that chose *K* to make its name memorable. The first talking movie featuring Mickey Mouse was *The Karnival Kid* in 1929.

In the twenty-first century, newspaper writers no longer indulge in spelling games with *K*, but its conspicuousness continues to be put to use in products like Kleenex, Kandy Korn hybrid sweet corn, and local businesses like the Kottage Kafe, Klassic Kar Detailers, and the Kute Kurl Beauty Salon.

The clownishness associated with the konspicuous *K*, however, deters its widespread use. So, for example, you can find a Kolorado Karaoke and Mobile DJ (the first *K* probably influenced by the spelling of the second word) and Kolorado Paint Kmpny, in Fort Collins, with one employee, but almost all of the thousands of Colorado businesses choose to spell Colorado with a *C*.

The sounds of OK were clearly secondary to its appearance in print, but they too are fortuitously clear and simple: two long vowels, *O* and *A*, separated in the middle by a quick *K*. Nearly every language in the world not only has these three sounds but allows them to be combined in that sequence, which accounts both for the spread of OK throughout the world and the penchant for discovering the "true" origin of OK in words or expressions of another language that sound very much like OK. Without its particular look and sound, OK might never have made it out of Boston.

FALSE ORIGINS

BEFORE PROCEEDING FURTHER, IT'S IMPORTANT TO CLEAR THE air about the origin of OK. Thanks to the published work of Allen Walker Read, who documented the emergence and spread of OK in 1839 and 1840 with literally hundreds of contemporary citations, it is absolutely clear that OK began as a joke in a Boston newspaper and was transformed by politics and a hoax into the expression we still use today. The trail of written evidence from that day to the present is thick and clear. No other origin is plausible. Yet throughout the history of OK there have been doubts. If it weren't for the overwhelming evidence, the true history of OK would indeed be hard to believe.

If you want to know only the facts about OK, you can skip this chapter. It is filled with untruths. They are untruths, however, that show the vitality of OK and the desire to bless it with a better beginning.

Say It Ain't So

"Personally I have a terrible time believing that a localized comical abbreviation fad invented the most familiar word in the world and did so without popularizing a single other abbreviation," says a discussant on the Wikipedia entry for OK. Indeed, it's almost an insult to our collective intelligence. We want nobler origins. No wonder so many other candidates have been proposed.

The first red herring was attribution of the initials OK to Andrew Jackson's misspelling of "all correct"—accurate in its interpretation of the abbreviation, but egregiously wrong about the inventor. As we have seen, that deliberate fiction was concocted when OK was barely a year old, in 1840. It was still a widely accepted explanation in October 1866, when journalist George Wakeman published an article on "Live Metaphors" in *The Galaxy: An Illustrated Magazine of Entertaining Reading* of New York City.

> But even this ["All serene!" his proposal for the call a night watchman should make] was neither as concise nor as satisfactory as the simple letters "O. K." All that anybody desired to know about anything that interested him was simply that it was "O. K." . . . They were a watchword of Tammany, were afterward used by the Whigs, and then became common property. They are supposed to mean "Oll Korrect," and the story is that General Andrew Jackson, who had more spirit than spelling, used to note this "O. K.," supposed by him the proper initials for the words, on the back of any paper which he found "all correct." But who knows whether this was not the sly contrivance of some polished Whig?

The Revolutionary OK

Wakeman was on the mark in doubting the Jackson origin of OK.
Having suspected one source, however, he holds the honor of pro-
moting another even more dubious:

> Some one has discovered an order-of-the-day of the old Revo-
> lutionary army, dated 6th September, 1780, in which the
> countersign is "O. K.," showing, if the order is genuine, that
> the letters were in use at that time.

Here is the "some one," from the *New-York Commercial Advertiser*
of December 6, 1841:

O.K.

> We have at length struck upon the origin of these mystical
> letters—stolen last year by the wicked Whigs, as their watch-
> words, from the sagamores of Tammany Hall. It will be seen
> from the heading of the following order that these letters
> formed the countersign of the guards on the 6th of September,
> 1780.
>   "HEAD Quarters, 6th Sept. 1780.
>   "Parole, RICHMOND. Counter-signs, {O.
>   {K.
> Watch-word—FABIUS.
> "For the Day, Brigadier Patterson,
> "Col. H. Jackson,
> "Col. Badlaw,
> "Brigade Major Nicholas Fish."

A document from half a century earlier! That would surely have
pride of place, upstaging the Boston joke of 1839. Except—

Even if this document is authentic, it hardly qualifies as a possible origin of the OK we know from fifty years later. For one thing, countersigns, as well as paroles and watchwords, are arbitrary and change daily. They are meant to be unknown to the enemy, so that might be an incentive to avoid a common phrase. For another, the *O* and *K* are listed on separate lines rather than next to each other. Finally, and most important, there is no subsequent chain of OKs leading from this instance to the widespread use of OK in 1839 and 1840. Even if someone took this isolated O.K. to mean "all correct," it subsequently vanished without a trace. The OK that appeared half a century later has no connection with these countersigns.

Young Andrew Jackson

It's not surprising, then, that little has been made of the O.K. countersigns of 1780. That was not true of a 1790 document published in an 1859 *History of Middle Tennessee* by one Albigence Waldo Putnam. Because of its documentary status and its connection with Andrew Jackson, it persuaded scholars for nearly a century to accept the false Jacksonian origin of OK. Twenty years after the emergence of OK in Boston, Putnam wrote:

> When General Jackson became candidate for President, it was published to the world that he spelled *all correct* "Oll Korrect," and the O.K. are familiar to everybody.
>
> We were startled to read the following record:
>
> "Wednesday, 6th Oct., 1790: Court met according to adjournment. Andrew Jackson, Esq., proved a bill of sale from Hugh McGary to Gasper Mansker for a negro man, which was O.K." These are the exact capital letters. We find another instance of this abbreviation, and two where the letters seem to be O.R.

Once again, there was no intermediate instance leading from these documents to the Boston newspaper of 1839, but the connection to Jackson made them hard to ignore. Finally, nearly a century later, researcher Woodford Heflin took a look at the originals. On close examination, it is evident that the letters on all of those documents actually are O.R., meaning "ordered recorded," not O.K. The capital letter that Putnam took for *K* is simply an *R* with a flourish. Careful scrutiny of the document in question showed that it actually reads, "Andrew Jackson, Esqr. proved a bill of Sale from Hugh McGary to Kasper Mansker for a negro man which is O.R." Heflin published a photograph of the document in the journal *American Speech* in 1941, to convince anyone who might doubt the correct interpretation.

So the search for OK in documents prior to 1839 has been fruitless, even with intense interest by scholars and now the vast new resources of searchable old books and periodicals available on the Internet. It is frankly doubtful that any credible antedatings of OK ever will be found, because if OK had been invented before 1839, we would expect not just an isolated instance but a succession of instances leading up to that year.

The lack of documentation hasn't deterred speculation, however, and speculation has often become belief. After all, the thinking goes, surely this greatest of Americanisms, known and used worldwide, must have had a more distinguished and logical origin than a joke in a newspaper.

The Intelligent Choctaw

W. S. Wyman of the University of Alabama, a professor of English, in 1885 and 1894 published articles arguing that the true origin of OK was the Choctaw language. This theory too involves

Andrew Jackson but gives him a more dignified reason for choosing to use OK. Wyman writes in his 1894 article,

> It is, however, probably true that General Jackson did indorse with the symbols O. K. public documents which he approved. General Jackson was no scholar, it is true, but he was not so ignorant as to think that "all correct" was spelled "oll korrect."
>
> If you will examine the autograph letters of General Jackson now in the archives of the Tennessee Historical Society, you will find that he could write fairly for a man who had small educational advantages in early life.
>
> The true explanation of O. K. is probably as follows: There is a tradition among the intelligent Choctaws of the old stock who once lived in Mississippi that General Jackson borrowed the expression O. K. from the Choctaw language.
>
> The Choctaws and the Chickasaws speak the same tongue. In the language of these two peoples there is no copulative verb that corresponds to "be" in English (*esse* in Latin). A substitute for this is found in the emphatic word *okéh*, which ends every assertion in Choctaw. An example will illustrate this.
>
> The English sentence, "The Choctaw Indian is a good fellow," would be in Choctaw, *Hattak uppeh hoomah chahtah achookmah okéh*, Man body red Choctaw good it-is-all-so. Here *okéh* serves as the verb of assertion. It means, "It is true," "It is so," "It is all right," etc.
>
> General Jackson was frequently among the Choctaws and Chickasaws before he became famous. He must have heard this expression often.
>
> He probably adopted it in early life as a very expressive kind of slang, and used it after he became President as a private symbol (O. K.) to indicate approval. . . .

> This theory of the origin of O. K. is, if not true, at least
> well invented, as the Italians say.

Professor Wyman then goes on to accept the authenticity of the
1790 document, explaining, "It is highly probable that this O. K.
in the record of the Sumner County Court is the very expression
used by Jackson to signify that the bill of sale was 'all right.'" We
now know that was all wrong.

Another scholar, Charles P. G. Scott, soon afterward added to
Wyman's explanation by asserting, "It seems probable that the
expression came into white men's notice in the Indian jargon
known in the 18th century and later as the 'Mobile' or 'Mobilian
trade language,' sometimes as the 'Chickasaw trade language,' the
Chickasaw being a dialect of the Choctaw." Conveniently, no trace
remains of that language.

Attractive as the Choctaw explanation is, there is no evidence
to support it, not even the 1790 document that now has been
disproved. To this day there is not a scrap of actual evidence that
OK had anything to do with Andrew Jackson.

But the Choctaw explanation was important all the same. It
appealed to scholars, in particular to the only Ph.D. who has ever
served as president of the United States, Woodrow Wilson. Without question, OK was a useful mark to make on a document, but
it would hardly be proper for a highly educated man to employ a
known misspelling. The Choctaw was a way out.

So President Wilson embraced the opportunity to give what
he assumed was proper historical respect to OK. He marked his
approval of documents not with OK but with *okeh*.

During Wilson's terms in office, that origin was also embraced,
or at least alluded to, by the OKeh label of phonograph records
(begun in 1915) and by an Okeh style of Arrow collars (begun in
1919).

OKeh Phonograph Record Label

Perhaps thanks to President Wilson, the *okeh* spelling maintained some currency with other writers. As late as 1948, the *St. Petersburg Times* had a front-page headline reading, "Senate Okeh of Truman's Program To Aid Backward Areas of World Forecast."

Many Initials

The letters *O* and *K* have long been in the English language. So naturally from time to time they have formed someone's initials. This coincidence has led to speculation that OK came from an exemplary product or service provided by an O.K.

One example was a biscuit supposedly provided to Union soldiers during the Civil War. According to a 1910 issue of the *Chicago Record-Herald*,

> When the Civil War broke out there existed in Chicago a firm of bakers known as O. Kendall & Sons, the head of the firm being Orrin Kendall. This firm immediately began the manufacture of army biscuit, and stamped them "O.K." to represent the firm. These biscuits, it is said, came to be preferred by the soldiers, who thought them a little better than the ordinary barmy bread. Soon "O.K." became a cant term of approval in the army and after the war it was carried into civil life and peace occupations.

The only problem with this theory, of course, is that OK was already flourishing more than twenty years before the Civil War. More likely, if there is truth in this story, the bakers drew on the affirmative connotation of OK rather than vice versa. For example, Pyle's O.K. Soap was already widely advertised before the Civil War began.

Half a century later another Chicago newspaper postulated an earlier biscuiteer as the source of OK. A letter to the *Chicago Tribune* published in 1957 declares:

> Sir:
>
> Here is the truth about O. K. In Boston about 1810 there was a baker named Otto Kimmel. He was very proud of his vanilla cookies, and the best ones he would ship down the Atlantic coast. These were stamped with his initials. Hence the term O. K. for anything that is perfect.
>
> FRANK BAINS

How someone in Chicago would know about a Boston baker a century and a half earlier wasn't explained. Nevertheless, this was enough of a possibility to prompt researcher Barry Popik to inquire at the Massachusetts Historical Society and the Boston Society for an Otto Kimmel of that era, but in vain; Kimmel wasn't even listed in the census.

How about a telegraph operator? Supposedly there was an Oscar Kent whose transmissions were so perfect that his sign-off, OK, became synonymous for *all correct*.

The website for the town of Kinderhook, New York, attributes OK to apples, again without any evidence beyond a crate at a present-day "eatery":

> There are many stories regarding the origins of the expression "O.K." One relates to the many apple orchards in the county. Back in the 1700s, apples from this area were packed in crates marked "Old Kinderhook." There is even one on display in one of the eateries on the village square. Apparently people started referring to them as "O.K." apples. Gradually the term was taken to mean a description of the apples' "good quality" rather than their location of origin!

One modern example using Kinderhook was proclaimed by none other than the soon-to-be-disgraced governor of New York, Eliot Spitzer, in February 2008. Speaking about Martin Van Buren's role in the building of the Erie Canal, he said:

> A little-known fact about Martin Van Buren: . . . He contributed a word to the English language. And that word is what we use every day and that word is OK. When Martin Van Buren was president and he wanted to get out of the White House he would put the initials OK on a memorandum and what it stood for was "Off to Kinderhook." That is the derivation of the word OK.

He got this from the *Encyclopedia of New York State*, and they ought to know. Right?

And then a modern biographer of Van Buren, Edward Widmer, told the *New York Times* that OK was "briefly short for 'oll korrect,' a Dutch phrase for 'all right,' but then got shifted onto Van Buren as he ran for President."

Many Languages

One reason OK has spread throughout the world, as we have noted, is that *O* and *K* are basic sounds found in most languages. Considering that languages have only a few dozen sounds (or letters) to form ten thousand or more words, it is likely that many languages will have combinations that sound like OK, either complete words such as Choctaw *okeh* or initials of words. It is also the case that English has borrowed many words from many other languages. It is a short jump from these facts to conclude that if a word in English sounds like something in another language, that expression in the other language must be the source of the English word. Choctaw and Mobile were just the first of many such candidates.

In turn, as OK has spread around the world, it is natural for speakers of other languages to assume that it developed from their own native expressions rather than being borrowed from American English.

Early in the twentieth century it was noticed that Aux Cayes, the French name of a port in Haiti, sounds a lot like OK. It was natural, then, to speculate that Aux Cayes was the source. But why? Some said it was the rum. Supposedly, a preferable sort of rum was exported from Aux Cayes, so sailors would say happily, "It's OK." But no one has found any documentation of this in the nineteenth century, let alone before 1839, and anyway there is no evidence that Aux Cayes rum really was renowned. An alternative says that it was Puerto Rican rum that was labeled Aux Quais. Or that it came from *aux quais,* "to the wharves," which is where French soldiers supposedly went during the American Revolution to find local women. Or that *au quai,* "to the dock," was used in New Orleans prior to the Louisiana Purchase of 1803 when a bale of cotton met an inspector's approval.

Yet another French possibility, rather far from the sound of OK but proposed in all seriousness, is that OK came from *bien coquet,* translated as "perfectly charming." Or it could have been *O qu-oui,* a hyperenthusiastic *oui* meaning "yes, indeed!" found in an eighteenth-century book.

Germanophiles have not been shy about proposing their language as the true origin of OK. One theory is that it was a misreading of the initials for *alles korrekt* written by a German military advisor during the Revolutionary War. Another more specifically attributes it to Baron von Steuben, the Prussian general who fought with the Americans in that war and supposedly wrote O.K. for *Ober-Kommando* next to his name. Or maybe it was *Oberst Kommandant.*

Other German candidates include *ohne Korrektur,* that is, "without correction [needed]," said to have been used on documents in the late nineteenth century.

Finnish offered *oikea* for "correct." Norwegian and Danish offered the abbreviation *H.G.,* pronounced "hah gay," supposedly meaning "ready for action."

Scots English *och aye,* translated "oh yes," is another serious candidate. So is Ulster English *ough aye,* with similar pronunciation and meaning.

The Greek language provides *olla kalla,* "all good" or "all right," as a candidate for OK. It was supposedly used by the Spartans in 600 B.C., as well as by Greek teachers on student papers in modern times. There is no doubt about the latter—but it was the result of importing OK from America, rather than exporting the earlier version. And apparently the Greek abbreviation, the letters omicron kappa (OK), means more than merely OK in English; it is said to be used for papers that are of high quality, "entirely good."

From Latin, *omnes korrecta* has been proposed.

African languages brought by slaves to the Americas have also been noticed as potential sources of OK. It could have come from *waw kay*, "yes indeed" in Wolof; *o ke*, "that's it" or "certainly" in Mandingo; or *ki*, an expression of surprise or satisfaction, in black Jamaican English, derived from Africa.

It could indeed. But like all other candidates from other languages, there is not a shred of evidence linking it to a Boston newspaper in March 1839.

OK / OKAY Already

What has all this speculation wrought? An enhancement of the image of OK, on one hand, as each claimant embraces our grand expression, and on the other hand a reduction to absurdity. The latter is evident in an art exhibit in New York City in the spring of 2005 with the title "OK / OKAY." The curator, Marc-Olivier Wahler, declares:

> The exhibition's curatorial point of departure is the disputed etymology of the terms OK and okay. Employed universally, both signify approval and assent or, when describing a quality, acceptability. The question of their origin, however, has sparked endless debates and inspired book-length treatises.

Maybe not endless, and maybe not book-length, but Waller does his best to widen the debate, listing eighteen different theories and democratically giving each equal weight. Among the theories not already mentioned above, there is the Civil War Theory:

> During the Civil War, when a battalion returned from the front, the first man in line carried a sign displaying the number of men killed in action: "9 Killed," "5 Killed," and so on. If the number was zero, the sign read OK, indicating that all had survived.

The Anglo-Saxon Theory:

> Several centuries before okay's first appearance, Norwegian and Danish sailors used the Anglo-Saxon term hogfor, meaning seaworthy. This was often abbreviated HG, pronounced hag-gay.

If Anglo-Saxon is too long ago, there was Old English Theory:

> In old England, the last harvest loads brought in from the fields were called hoacky or horkey. The same term also denoted the feast following the harvest and, thus, indicated its satisfactory completion. It was soon shortened to OK.

The Shipbuilder Theory:

> Early shipbuilders marked the timber they prepared. The first to be laid was marked OK Number 1, short for Outer Keel Number 1.

The British Parliament Theory:

> Some bills going through the House of Lords required the approval of Lords Onslow and Kilbracken. After reading and approving these bills, they would both initial them, producing the combined signature OK.

Another Greek Theory:

> According to the text Geoponica, dated 920 CE, the Greek
> letters omega and khi, when repeated twice, are effective as a
> magical incantation against fleas.

And the Indian Chief Theory:

> Keokuk, Iowa, is named for an Indian chief. His admirers
> sometimes remarked, "Old Keokuk, he's all right"; the initials
> OK came to mean the same thing.

In any case, what's the relevance to the exhibition? Wahler explains:

> Suggesting that issues of translation can challenge standard
> assumptions, the artists in OK / OKAY make artworks that stand
> out in a pragmatic world that tends to value clarity and brevity.

As it turns out, there was no need to worry about clarity and brev-
ity at the two locations of the "OK / OKAY" show. Instead, the
curator explains,

> The shows explore the myriad ways in which art is no longer
> defined by position or place—instead gliding over the visible
> and exposing the limitless strata comprising its structure.
> Wahler proposes that this interplay triggers a slippage in inter-
> pretations as well as constant oscillations between different
> languages. It is in this unstable field, he suggests, that contem-
> porary art finds its meaning: not as a cultural domain in search
> of aesthetic definitions, but rather a true dynamic.

Got it? And if there was one element that those works of art by the
dozen exhibitors had in common, as displayed on the exhibition
website, it was that they made no reference whatever to OK.

Which is an appropriate ending for this chapter. It has added nothing to the true explanation of OK's origins in Chapters 3, 4, and 5. But if you have read through all of these conjectures, you deserve a license of your own. You are free to use your own creativity in imagining a properly dignified, colorful, or important origin for OK. Just be aware that it has nothing to do with what actually happened.

THE BUSINESS
OF OK

WITHIN A FEW YEARS AFTER ITS BIRTH IN 1839 AND TUMULTUOUS participation in the presidential campaign of 1840, OK developed surprisingly sober uses. Not only was it employed, in all seriousness, to approve hard copies of documents, but it also was used for their electronic versions. Indeed, it appears that OK was put to electronic use almost as soon as electronic use—the telegraph, back in those days—was born.

The telegraph, the railroad, and OK all were in their infancy in the 1840s. By midcentury, scarcely a decade after the first instance of OK, the three were permanently intertwined in serious business. OK was no longer just a joke.

The joke hadn't disappeared, to be sure. Awareness of OK as a misspelled abbreviation for "all correct," whether in its Boston

origin or in the widely retold myth of President Jackson's notation on
documents, remained strong, encouraging its use in joking contexts
and inhibiting widespread use in literature. But when it came to the
telegraph and railroad, the joke was ignored. OK was just too useful.

Telegraphic OK

The birth of OK coincided with the birth of the telegraph. Samuel
F. B. Morse demonstrated his electric telegraph in 1838, a year
before OK. In 1843, four years after OK was born, Congress appro-
priated $30,000 for an experimental line between Washington and
Baltimore. In 1844 the first long-distance message, "What hath
God wrought," was transmitted in Morse code, followed later that
year by the first news from Baltimore, of the nomination of Henry
Clay as Whig candidate for president.

Those first messages did not include OK. But a decade later,
telegraph wires had extended in many directions, and they had
caught up with the railroads, which were doing likewise. The company that would be known as Western Union was formed in 1851,
linking smaller telegraph companies together; in 1861 its famous
transcontinental line was completed. Meanwhile, also in 1851, railroads began dispatching trains by telegraph. For mutual benefit,
telegraph lines usually ran next to the rails.

And it was there that OK became SOP. Evidence as to exactly
when that happened is elusive, but in an 1861 book published in
Columbus, Ohio, *Reminiscences in the Life of a Locomotive Engineer*, it was already referred to as an established practice. Looking
back at the early days of railroading and the dangers railroad men
routinely faced, the anonymous engineer recalls:

> If one of his intimate companions gets killed, he can
> only bestow a passing thought upon it, for he has not been

unexpectant of it, and he knows full well that the same accident may at the same place make it his turn next, as he passes over the same road every day, running the same chances, as did his friend just gone.

I had, while I was on the H—— road, a particular friend, an engineer. We were inseparable, and were both of us, alike, given to fits of despondency, at which times we would, with choking dread, bid each other farewell, and "hang around" the telegraph office to hear the welcome "O K" from the various stations, signifying that our trains had passed "on time" and "all right."

Over nineteenth-century telegraph wires OK would have been sent in the original Morse code, also known as American Morse or Railroad Morse, in the pattern dot-gap-dot dash-dot-dash, rather than dash-dash-dash dash-dot-dash of today's International Morse Code. The *O* was signaled by two dots with a long intracharacter gap to distinguish it from *I*, which used two dots with a short intracharacter gap.

Just a decade after the locomotive engineer's reminiscences, telegraph communications showing extensive use of OK were transcribed in a book complaining of inappropriate use of Western Union wires by the government's Signal Office in Washington, D.C. "It can hardly fail to excite surprise that the Signal Office should interrupt and suspend the business of the public on the great commercial lines of the country during the most active hours of the day with such trifling matters," the authors complain. Here are some samples they use as evidence:

CONVERSATIONS AUGUST 7, 1871

Signal Office to Boston.—The Secretary of War asks, "What is the weather and thermometer? Is Observer about there? Tell him yourself, if not."

Boston to Signal Office.—"Weather hazy—pleasant—East. Don't know about thermometer."

Signal Office to Boston.—"Thanks of the Secretary of War. O. K."

Signal Office to Chicago.—"Is S. or G. there?"

Chicago to Signal Office.—"Who do you want?"

Signal Office to Chicago.—"Is S. or G. there?"

Chicago to Signal Office.—"Yes, wait a minute. I'll get them."

Signal Office to Chicago.—"Good morning. The Secretary of War is here again. Are you working through to San Francisco? Can you put West on for a minute?"

Chicago to Signal Office.—"West O. K., can put it on here, but it will be slow work. I can repeat it quicker than you can work through, and make it appear as though you were working direct. Won't that do?"

Signal Office to Chicago.—"He has nothing important to say. Only wanted to see if wires would work. He has been trying the Franklin lines, but there is not much show for them."

Chicago to Signal Office.—"I'll put it on if you think best; but this is the very worst time of day for our business."

Signal Office to Chicago.—"Let it go till some other day."

Chicago to Signal Office.—"Suppose you arrange for to-morrow morning, say 10.30, Washington time, then I will have every thing ready. I am short of wires and crowded with business now."

Signal Office to Chicago.—"O. K. Will let you know. 12:30."

AUGUST 9, 1871

Chicago to Signal Office.—"Who are you calling?"

Signal Office to Chicago.—"Is Cheyenne and Corinne [Utah] here?"

> *Chicago to Signal Office.*—"Yes."
>
> *Corinne to Chicago.*—"Do you want us?"
>
> *Chicago to Corinne.*—"Yes. Washington is here, and wants you. Answer him."
>
> *Signal Office to Corinne.*—"Please give the Secretary of War the state of the weather."
>
> *Corinne to Signal Office.*—"Little hazy. Thermometer 75."
>
> *Signal Office to Corinne.*—"O. K."

In 1876 a *Manual of Telegraphy, Designed for Beginners,* by a Professor J. E. Smith, explains the practice:

> One office desiring to communicate with another, makes the call of that station three our four times, then gives his own office signal, and keeps repeating this until he receives a reply, or gets tired of calling.
>
> An office answering a call makes the letter I two or three times, more or less, then its own call.
>
> An acknowledgment of the receipt of any kind of communication is made by returning O K, followed by the call of the office receiving the communication.
>
> Writing one's own office call is termed *signing;* and this must be done *once* and *only* once, at the close of everything that is written over a line, be it calling, answering calls, giving O K, sending messages, or conversing.
>
> An acknowledgment of the receipt of any kind of communication is made by returning O K, followed by the call of the office receiving the communication.

Smith gives an example of a message from Boston:

> In acknowledging the receipt of a dispatch, Boston replies with O K B, or sometimes precedes the O K with the letter I a few times.

No communication is ever sent until the office to receive it has been called, and a reply has been returned; and no message is ever regarded as transmitted until the office receiving it gives O K, or commences to send back other dispatches.

The Atlantic Cable

The laying of a telegraph cable across the Atlantic, from Ireland to Newfoundland, was also marked with OK. In July 1865, in the midst of laying the cable, the *Great Eastern* sent this telegram to shore:

The cable is all O. K. again. The signals are perfect. A small fault was discovered and cut out. The *Great Eastern* is now paying out the cable in latitude 52 degrees, longitude 12 degrees.

A week later that cable broke. But in 1866 the *Great Eastern* tried again with a new cable and managed to salvage the old one as well. A British chronology of major events of 1866, telling of this successful voyage, included a technical explanation of OK for its English audience:

But what of the electrical condition of the cable during this period? Simply through its entire length it was perfect, or, as it is technically called, O.K. (all correct).

OK on the Moon

Although it would take another century before Americans actually landed on the moon, OK was already put to lunar use in a science fiction story by Edward Everett Hale published in the *Atlantic*

Monthly in 1870 and 1871. The moon of this story was an artificial satellite, a "brick moon" accidentally launched with people aboard and circling the earth at an altitude of five thousand miles. Responding to a message delivered literally in leaps and bounds in Morse code by the thirty-seven people on the brick moon, using huge strips of black crepe,

> Haliburton showed the symbols for "I understand," but he could not resist also displaying . . — . —, which are the dots and lines to represent O. K., which, he says, is the shortest message of comfort. And not having exhausted the space on the Flat, he and Robert, before night closed in, made a gigantic O. K., fifteen yards from top to bottom, and in marks that were fifteen feet through.
>
> After a pause, the united line of leapers resumed their jumps and hops. Long and short spelled out:—
>
> "Your O. K. is twice as large as it need be."

A century later, on July 20, 1969, it could be argued that the first word spoken when the first humans actually landed on the moon was not Neil Armstrong's "Houston, Tranquility Base here. The Eagle has landed" but rather, fifteen seconds earlier, Buzz Aldrin's "OK. Engine stop." In any case, Armstrong's second statement after landing was "OK, let's get on with it. OK, we're going to be busy for a minute." (A transcript of the full conversation appears in Chapter 13.)

OK for a Bribe

Further evidence of the business use of OK comes from details of shady business conducted by General William W. Belknap, secretary of war in the early 1870s. Apparently in gratitude for kindness to his wife when she was ill, in 1870 Secretary Belknap gave C. P. Marsh of New York City the position of post trader at Fort Sill in Indian Territory. Marsh, however, immediately asked that the appointment be given to John S. Evans, who was one of the actual traders at Fort Sill. In return for the exclusive franchise, Evans agreed to pay $12,000 a year to Marsh, and Marsh kindly sent half of that amount to Secretary Belknap, at first supposedly to help his wife, who died soon after, then supposedly to help the secretary's child, who also died, and then just for the general himself. This was the cause of an impeachment trial in the Senate. In the record of the trial there are two references to the use of OK by the secretary. Marsh stated that when he sent the first remittance to Belknap, "the defendant [Belknap] admitted the receipt by an 'O. K.'" Senator E. G. Lapham, in his summary of the case, said that later payments omitted that acknowledgment:

> The General did not even respond as when the money was sent by express or mail with an "O. K." This, I suppose, is one of the military ciphers used during the war by General Belknap. It certainly had a higher signification than that placed upon it by the ordinary Yankee, because it was used by a high official and dignified cabinet officer. Marsh was not asked, and it does not appear when the payments were made to the defendant personally whether he gave a wink or a nod or graciously smiled upon his benefactor. The probability is that after counting the money and ascertaining that the amount was correct he simply said "O. K."

The use of OK in a formal report was rare enough to merit quotation marks around OK, as well as the witticism about its being a military cipher, but it is clear that it was well known and routinely used.

Bookkeeping

Another glimpse of the business use of OK appears in *Business Bookkeeping,* published in 1894. Regarding branch store accounts, *Business Bookkeeping* instructs:

> After checking the bills for such goods, to see that they are O. K. (all correct), the branch store turns the bills over to the main store, first debiting "Merchandise" and crediting "Main Store."

OK Blanks

Meanwhile, to keep track of everything, by the early twentieth century railroads had developed OK blanks. Theodore Dreiser made OK blanks a focus of his autobiographical 1919 story "The Mighty Rourke," telling of his experience years earlier working for the Irish foreman Rourke on the railroad:

> When I first met him he was laying the foundation for a small dynamo in the engine-room of the repair shop at Spike. . . .
>
> [He] fished out of the pocket of his old gray coat a soiled and crumpled letter, which he carefully unfolded with his thick, clumsy fingers. Then he held it up and looked at it defiantly.
>
> "I waant ye to go to Woodlawn," he continued, "an' look after some bolts that arre up there—there's a keg av thim—an' sign the bill fer thim, an' ship thim down to me. An' thin I waant ye to go down to the ahffice an' take thim this o.k." Here again he fished around and produced another crumpled slip, this time of a yellow color (how well I came to know them!), which I soon learned was an o.k. blank, a form which

had to be filled in and signed for everything received, if no more than a stick of wood or a nail or a bolt. The company demanded these of all foremen, in order to keep its records straight. Its accounting department was useless without them. At the same time, Rourke kept talking of the "nonsinse av it," and the "onraisonableness" of demanding o.k.s for everything. "Ye'd think some one was goin' to sthale thim from thim," he declared irritably and defiantly.

Dreiser took the OK blank to the "ahffice."

There I found the chief clerk, a mere slip of a dancing master in a high collar and attractive office suit, who was also in a high state of dudgeon because Rourke, as he now explained, had failed to render an o.k. for this and other things, and did not seem to understand that he, the chief clerk, must have them to make up his reports. Sometimes o.k.s did not come in for a month or more, the goods lying around somewhere until Rourke could use them. He wanted to know what explanation Rourke had to offer, and when I suggested that the latter thought, apparently, that he could leave all consignments of goods in one station or another until such time as he needed them before he o.k.ed for them, he fairly foamed.

Rourke responds to the clerk's request for an OK blank:

"An o.k. blank! An o.k. blank!" he echoed contentiously, but in a somewhat more conciliatory spirit. "He wants an o.k. blank, does he? Well, I expect ye might as well give thim to him, thin. I think the man lives on thim things, the way he's aalways caallin' fer them. Ye'd think I was a bookkeeper an' foreman at the same time; it's somethin' aaful. An o.k. blank! An o.k. blank!" and he sputtered to silence.

A little while later he humorously explained that he had "clane forgot thim, anyhow."

OK Ballot

Joe Chapple's election-year biography of Warren G. Harding, published in 1920, amid a heap of bloviation refers to OK on ballots:

> The real biography of Warren G. Harding will be written day by day, in act and deed under the pitiless spotlight of a Presidential campaign. Every word, every inflection, almost every inner thought, is X-rayed by the earnest voter of the country seeking to get the truth concerning the man whose name will appear on over twenty million ballots—the white messengers of authority—scattered over the country like snowflakes on November 2, 1920, on which the voters of the United States are to register with a simple mark of "X" or O.K. with a lead pencil, the measure of the man whom they choose to have as their President to safeguard the interest of home and country while the mad tides of internationalism are threatening our own and other shores.

OK Products

In contrast with its pervasive use in the conduct of business operations, OK has never enjoyed widespread use as a product name. This is for the same reason that a book of famous OK quotations would be so short. OK is just . . . OK. It is affirmative but value neutral. It affirms that something is satisfactory, but not that it stands out in any way from its peers. Would Satisfactory Soup sell? Would customers flock to a Satisfactory Coffee Shop? Would they book with a Satisfactory Travel Agency? Neither would they be stirred to patronize OK Soup, OK Coffee, or OK Travel.

Still, there are exceptions. OK may be good enough when the implication is that competitors are not. This may be the reason that the very first soap powder manufactured in the United States was called O.K. It was manufactured in New York City by James Pyle, beginning in the late 1850s. By 1862, when the *New York Times* ran this ad, it was the nation's leading soap:

> THE BEST SOAP IN USE. JAMES PYLE'S O. K. SOAP.
>
> Every housekeeper that tries it uses no other. It not only lessens labor, but, being pure and hard, will go much further than ordinary Soap. It is good for the Toilet, for Shaving, and just the thing for washing Muslins and laces. One pound will make three gallons of good Soft-Soap. In fact, no other Soap is required about the house when PYLE'S O. K. SOAP is in use. The most intelligent classes in New-York use it. Editors of most of the religious papers patronize it. Editors of the *N. Y. Tribune* and *Evening Post* use it, and everybody will when they have tried it.
>
> PYLE'S SALERATUS and CREAM TARTAR are also the most popular of any in use, deservedly so.
>
> Sold by grocers everywhere. Manufactured corner of Washington and Franklin sts., New-York.

An 1871 ad in *Harper's Weekly* took aim at competitors, implying that they were not OK:

PYLE'S O. K. SOAP.

Good Soap is the desideratum of every economical house-keeper, yet the market is flooded with that which has the semblance, but not the qualities of real soap; and consumers thereof unconsciously incur an extravagant expenditure in the course of time. Pyle's "O.K." is a pure article, the economy of which has been thoroughly established.

In 1877 an ad in the *Times* put it more succinctly:

PYLE'S O. K. SOAP

Renders house-cleaning easy and complete, in half the usual time. Sold by grocers everywhere.

After the success of O.K. Soap, Pyle also introduced Pearline, which was to become the leading laundry soap of the era. Pearline must have been better than O.K., at least as a brand name. Pyle later sold the O.K. brand to Procter and Gamble, which continued to manufacture O.K. Soap until the 1940s. Perhaps the customers of O.K. soap were people who doubted soap could be better than satisfactory.

A Livery in Tombstone

Undoubtedly the most famous OK business in the nineteenth century, however, and the only one whose name remains famous in the twenty-first century, was a stable in a dusty little town in Arizona Territory. It would have escaped the notice of history except for a gunfight that took place in the neighborhood on October 26, 1881. As is well known to history and legend, the three Earp brothers and Doc Holliday battled five "cowboys" seeking revenge on them, and three of the cowboys were killed.

The O.K. Corral, Livery, and Feed Stable was established in Tombstone in February 1879. Was it named after the proprietor? No, his name was John Montgomery, not Otto Krummholz. There seems to be no record of why Montgomery chose O.K., so it is simply assumed that he made use of a well-known label. It may well be that other stables in Arizona Territory were less than OK.

The gunfight did not actually take place at Montgomery's stable, but that was where the cowboys had spent the afternoon before the shooting. Perhaps that was why the gunfight has been associated with the O.K. Corral. Perhaps also O.K. was more memorable than Fly's Lodging House and Photographic Studio, where the gunfight began, or Fremont Street, where it ended.

$1.38 for Penrod

The inability of OK to convey an edge over competing products, to assert more than "satisfactory," is implicitly satirized in Booth Tarkington's *Penrod*, a popular humorous novel, published in 1914, about an eleven-year-old:

> There was a partially defaced sign upon the front wall of the box; the donjon-keep had known mercantile impulses:
>
> > The O. K. RaBiT Co.
> > PENROD ScHoFiELD AND CO.
> > iNQuiRE FOR PricEs
>
> This was a venture of the preceding vacation, and had net-ted, at one time, an accrued and owed profit of $1.38. Prospects had been brightest on the very eve of cataclysm. The

storeroom was locked and guarded, but twenty-seven rabbits and Belgian hares, old and young, had perished here on a single night—through no human agency, but in a foray of cats, the besiegers treacherously tunnelling up through the sawdust from the small aperture which opened into the stall beyond the partition. Commerce has its martyrs.

OK Chevrolet

In the right context, however, even in the twentieth century OK could find a commercial use. Chevrolet succeeded for a time by linking OK specifically to the OK mark used on documents. In the mid twentieth century, Chevrolet dealers literally tagged their used cars with OK. It was an apt choice. To claim that a new car was OK would hardly interest buyers, but the customer's number one concern about a used car was "Is it OK?"

Chevrolet dealers put on their used cars a red tag declaring "This is an OK USED CAR," featuring OK in large bright red lowercase script, with a narrow blue shadow, on a yellow background surrounded by a blue circle. Dealers displayed a large sign with that OK design, and it appeared frequently in magazine advertisements. "Buy a used car with this tag . . . and buy with NEW CAR confidence!" reads an ad from 1954. "Look for this tag and get a used car you can believe in," reads another.

A full-page 1965 magazine ad, illustrated with the OK sign, reads:

> "We go out of our way to welcome you when you're looking for your first used car.
>   We're Chevy dealers."

You wouldn't be surprised to hear this at your Chevrolet dealer's.

At a Chevy dealer's, you get the treatment he hopes brings you back next time you're looking for a used car. Or even a new car.

He'll also welcome you with many different late-model trade-ins. As well as experienced used car salesmen who actually wait on you, once you've looked the cars over.

And because Chevrolet dealers go out of their way for you, you don't have to go out of your way for them. You'll find at least one—complete with after-the-sale service facilities—right in your neighborhood. . . .

Chevrolet was the economy division of General Motors, below Buick, Oldsmobile, and Cadillac, so it is no accident that it was Chevrolet that advertised the even greater economy of buying a used car. It was . . . OK.

Chevrolet long ago retired the OK tag, but there are present-day used car dealers who use memories of the Chevrolet campaign to advantage, including OK Used Cars of St. Louis, established 1992, which advertises: "Offering late model vehicles that are serviced and safety checked before they are offered for sale. We offer on or off site vehicle inspections with the service facility of your choice." The logo of OK Used Cars includes the red script *ok* on a yellow background in a blue circle just like Chevrolet's.

Why would OK work for used cars but not, say, wedding receptions? Well, a buyer's concern about a used car is that it's OK, that it doesn't have serious problems. Adjectives like *wonderful* and *great* for a used car raise suspicions. For a used car, OK seems a more honest claim. A wedding reception, on the other hand, had better be better than OK.

Not So OK Soda

The peril of using OK in a product name, even as a joke, was demonstrated by the Coca-Cola company in the mid-1990s when it test-marketed a product known as OK Soda. The company's marketing department supposedly determined that OK was the best-known expression among all the world's languages, and Coke was second best. They even go together: OK is Coke's middle name (or letters). It's possible that the worldwide success of Coke, like that of OK, involved the distinctive letters *O* and *K* and their sounds. But recognition does not necessarily mean enthusiasm.

And that information turned out to be irrelevant, anyhow. The company decided to name its product OK Soda, not OK Coke, and it was tested not all over the world but just in various locations in the United States.

The company and its ad agency were aware that OK wouldn't add zest to the drink. Curiously, that seemed to be the point. OK Soda, made of cola enhanced with fruit flavors, was designed to appeal to teenagers, especially boys. And teenagers, the thinking went, were too cynical for ordinary advertising pitches. So the quirky advertising for OK Soda went so far as to disparage the product, with declarations like "Never overestimate the remarkable abilities of OK brand soda." An "OK Manifesto" included other lukewarm sayings:

What's the point of OK? Well, what's the point of anything?

The better you understand something, the more OK it turns out to be.

OK Soda does not subscribe to any religion, or endorse any political party, or do anything other than feel OK.

There is no real secret to feeling OK.

> **Please wake up every morning knowing that things are
> going to be OK.**

Some of these lines were allusions to the "I'm OK, you're
OK" psychology of two decades earlier, but that did not negate
the lukewarm connotation of OK, and the allusions were elusive
anyhow.

Coca-Cola even tried to get its term *OK-ness* added to the dictionary, with this definition: "An optimistic feeling that in spite of
the complications of day-to-day life, things always work themselves out." But you can't change the meaning of a word by fiat,
even the fiat of the world's largest soft drink company. OK was
satisfactory, no question, but not intrinsically optimistic or
encouraging. "Think OK, drink OK" was another of OK Soda's
slogans. Not exactly electrifying.

OK Today

OK permeates our documentation and conversation, our personal
and business lives—and yet it remains practically nonexistent in
the names of products and rare in the names of businesses. OK
affirms, but without the enthusiasm that a product or business
would want.

A search for present-day OK businesses, therefore, even with
the vacuuming power of Google, turns up little. One category
with a few OKs is the barbershop. There is OK Barber in down-
town Grants Pass, Oregon, with the oldest barber in the state.
There are OK Barber Shops in Rochester, New York, and Rochester, Minnesota, as well as Millbrooks, Alabama, among many
others. Of the OK Barber Shop in Red Bluff, California, a
reviewer says,

This is the normal old time 1950s barber shop. It is not for people wanting a salon style haircut or something that is more modern in terms of styling. It is a place for an older gentleman who still wears his Marine Corp style haircut. I have found that in general they cut hair much too short. Their perception of short is different than other places that I have used to get a haircut. If that is the kind of haircut you want, than this is a place you can go to.

For some men, a haircut just needs to be OK. You can get an old-fashioned haircut of that kind at an OK barber.

A barbershop can be OK and even advertise itself as such, but there are no OK Stylists and only one OK Salon, in Long Beach, California. It too seems old-fashioned, according to reviewer Judy K.:

> Need a good haircut. Don't have much money or want to waste a lot of time having it done then go to O K Salon. It's a very small place at the edge of the shopping center next to Yum Yum Donuts. Don't expect coffee and glamour here but you will get a good cut from any of the stylists. I can't speak about coloring, perms, manicures or other services because I've only had my haircut here.

With this one exception, you'd have to go as far as Chandigarh, India, to find an OK Salon and Academy.

A few beauty salons, to be sure, take the name OK. There are OK Beauty Salons in New Llano, Louisiana, and in Longmont, Colorado, where you can get wedding dresses and bridal gowns; the Han OK Beauty Salon in Flushing, New York; OK Beauty Salon & Boutique in Cheyenne, Wyoming; the Korean-American OK Beauty Salon in Anchorage, Alaska (cross listed under Adult Entertainment, for some reason); and the OK Beauty Salon in

Anaheim, California, where Bao Trang Nguyen and Lucie Nguyen are the operators, Quang Knguyen is a manicurist, and Tuyet Mai T Vu is a cosmetologist. What most of these have in common is a language other than English spoken by their proprietors. In other languages, the American import OK has a more exotic connotation than in American English. Then too, OK is as American an expression as you can find, so OK may be as much a gesture of Americanism as displaying a flag.

You can find an OK Bakery in Centreville, Virginia, and in the Bensonhurst neighborhood of Brooklyn, New York. To judge by reviewers' comments about the latter, the inadvertent implication of mediocrity is apt:

> Am not sure why any establishment would willingly brand itself as mediocre, but I will write this off as being lost-in-translation. Then again, this is your standard Chinese Bakery quality: no more, no less.

> This place lives up to its name, its just Ok.

> Decent breads, coffee, once had a taro bubble tea which was not that bad.

> They have some cakes which arent very good lol as well as some dim sum and noodles in the back.

The one exception to the scarcity of OK companies is dry cleaners. For some reason there are hundreds of OK Cleaners throughout the country. Maybe it's because all we ask from cleaners is that they return our clothes in OK condition, no worse than they were before. Maybe it's because too many cleaners turn out not to be OK, and customers need reassurance that their cleaner is OK. Maybe it's because some cleaners are operated by people who experience the excitement of OK in languages other than English. In any case, OK Cleaners are found in places ranging from El Monte, California, to Naperville, Illinois, Lithia Springs, Georgia, and Collegeville, Pennsylvania. There is OK Cleaners and Alterations in Lakewood, Washington, and OK Cleaners and Shoe Service is in Hudson, Ohio.

O.K. CLUBS

WHILE OK WAS WORKING ON THE RAILROAD, OVER THE TELE-
graph lines, on documents, and even occasionally in the names of
companies and products, it wasn't forgotten in one of its important original uses. The political OK Clubs of 1840 were not revived
for later presidential elections, but the idea of labeling a club OK
caught on. Well into the turn of the twentieth century, OK Clubs
flourished throughout the nation.

After OK had been adopted as the name of a club by the Tammany boys in the presidential election of 1840, others happily followed suit. This might have been because OK was instantly
recognizable yet satisfyingly mysterious. It had connotations of
success—after all, by midcentury OK was used to approve documents and confirm arrangements by telegraph—but also of fun,

considering the absurdity of the well-known misspelling of "all correct," and even of mystery, considering the many possible joking interpretations OK could evoke.

During the Civil War there were OK Boys, at least in North Carolina. An 1867 narrative of the Civil War by Augustus Woodbury says of the Confederate forces on Roanoke:

> There were infantry and artillery on the island. There were the "Overland Greys," "Yankee Killers," "Sons of Liberty," "Jackson Avengers," "O. K. Boys," from North Carolina, and some, with a more respectable name, from Virginia.

To Woodbury, apparently, OK lacked a little in respectability.

New York City remained a center of OK Club activity. Consider this description of a parade there on the eve of the 1888 presidential election, a dispatch published in the November 5 *Fort Worth Daily Gazette*:

NEW YORK'S LATEST RALLY.

> New York, Nov. 4—The Democratic paraders last night were fantastically decorated and bedecked with flags and bandanas in every conceivable way. They moved along twelve abreast, but were frequently blocked by the crushing crowd whom it seemed the police were powerless to handle. Everywhere could be heard the question: "What's the matter with Grover?" [Cleveland, the Democratic candidate for president] and regularly came the answer "He's all right." . . .
>
> Then came the Commercial "O K" Club, the glass trade men, the wholesale dry goods porters and truckmen, retail dry goods clerks, the Stock Exchange Club, auxilliary club of the same, Consolidated Stock Exchange, Summer Guards, Railroad Club, West Side Business Men's Club, wholesale

jewelers, insurance men, custom house brokers, photographers, wholesale druggists, hide and leather, boot and shoe men, Young Men's Independent Club and the Elevated Railroad employees.

On March 29, 1900, an OK Club made front-page news in the *New-York Tribune* for a different reason:

MAN'S BODY FOUND IN THE BAY.
BELIEVED TO BE THAT OF CAPTAIN CHARLES BARRY

The body of a drowned man was found yesterday in New-York Bay. A letter addressed to T. S. Shortland, No. 110 Wall-st., New-York, was found on him. There was also a receipt from the O. K. Club for $1 dues. T. S. Shortland, of the Shortland Brothers' Transportation Company, 110 Wall-st., when asked as to the letter, said that he thought it probable the body was that of Captain Charles Barry, a former employee of the company. "He has not been in our employ since January," he added, "but I understand he has been missing for some time. The fact that he had the card of the O. K. Club proves him to have been an employee of this firm, for that is the name of a benevolent organization our men have."

OK Clubs weren't confined to New York, however, but flourished far and wide. Baltimore, for example, had a "juvenile literary society" called the O.K. Club, whose letter of praise for *Appletons' Journal* appeared in an 1871 issue of that publication. After quoting the club's endorsement ("We consider it the best family paper now published in this country"), the editors comment: "These are obviously very judicious views, and we cordially congratulate the young gentlemen of the O. K. Club on their good taste and sound judgment. They are certainly O. K. about the JOURNAL."

And there were many other clubs. Page 10 of the *St. Paul Daily Globe* for September 16, 1888, carried this announcement: "The O. K. club will give a dance at Thomas hall Saturday evening, Sept. 22." The *Sacramento Record-Union* of May 5, 1891, reported on page 3 that "The D. C. O. K. club will give a dance at Liberty Gardens, Highland Park, on Thursday evening." (No explanation for D. C., but the O. K. part of the club name has to bring OK to mind.)

In the *Richmond* (Va.) *Times* for May 26, 1901, on page 5 we read: "The O. K. Club will give a picnic on to-morrow at Portiwiag Farm. The wagons will leave 622 Louisiana at 9 A.M." And in Falls City, Nebraska, the *Tribune* announced on January 17, 1908, page 4: "The O. K. club gave a party Tuesday night at the home of Ed Davis and wife. Games were played and enjoyable evening passed by the young people. Oysters were served."

The Harvard OK

OK even went to college. The taint of Tammany did not deter OK from entering the arena of high culture at the nation's oldest institution of higher education, Harvard College.

On September 27, 1858, nearly two decades after the invention of OK, fifteen members of the Harvard Class of 1859 founded a literary society with the name OK. Formed in opposition to the Greek fraternity system at Harvard, the OK took as its quite serious aim the promotion of elocution and literature. The OK met every two weeks that academic year. According to research by Christian J. W. Kloesel, published a century later in the *New England Quarterly,*

> During regular meetings a paper on the exercises of the previous meeting was presented by an appointed editor; six appointed declaimers offered their appraisals and introduced

new matters of literary interest; and the remaining members
joined in declamations and other exercises.

Since the members were graduating seniors, the Harvard OK
would have expired with their graduation in 1859, but that spring
they adopted a new constitution admitting four members from
the junior class in addition to the seniors, thus ensuring continu-
ation of the OK.

An example of the high standards of the OK appears in a
memorial biography of one Francis Custis Hopkinson, published
in 1866:

> He was strong in debate, taking front rank in the "Institute";
> and his manly oratory always won for him admiration in the
> "O.K."

The Harvard OK continued until the midst of World War I in
1916 or 1917, with ups and downs both in membership and in seriousness of purpose. In the 1870s, for example, Edward S. Martin
later recalled:

> The O. K. was the literary Society. At it we read papers and
> consumed beer and little cakes cut in the form of O and K.

But for most of its lifetime the OK remained focused on literary declamations and exercises. And its members included many
who went on to illustrious careers, not the least of them Ernest L.
Thayer, author of "Casey at the Bat," and President Theodore
Roosevelt. If the expression OK had lacked a little in respectability
because of its association with low humor and New York politics,
the company of the Harvard OK helped raise its status.

But what did that OK stand for? It was one of the Harvard
club's most closely kept secrets, but Kloesel discovered in a letter

from one of the founding members to another that it stood for "Orthoepy Klub." *Orthoepy* is a ten-dollar word for "proper pronunciation," and Klub is another not-so-klever misspelling in the tradition of Korrekt. (That explains why it was always referred to as "the OK" rather than redundantly "the OK Club.") There's an undergraduate sense of humor in pairing an elegant word with a misspelled simple one.

THE LITERARY OK

THE HUMOR OF OK, ITS POLITICAL RELEVANCE, AND ITS everyday use in commerce and clubs might portend its widespread use in literature of the later part of the nineteenth century. Such, strangely enough, is not the case. The great American authors of the later nineteenth century, and the near-great, have one thing in common: They all avoid OK.

You will search in vain for OK in the pages of Emerson, Hawthorne, Longfellow, Whittier, Poe, and Holmes. Perhaps that's not too surprising; although all of them lived at least a decade after OK was invented, all were born before 1809 and would have been in their thirties before they first had the opportunity to learn of it.

Younger, in their twenties in 1839 at the time of the birth of OK, were Margaret Fuller, Harriet Beecher Stowe, Richard Henry Dana, Henry David Thoreau, Frederick Douglass, James Russell Lowell, Herman Melville, and Walt Whitman. Still no OKs, though these include the authors of *Uncle Tom's Cabin* and *Song of Myself*, works that easily might have included OK.

(Edward Everett Hale, a once influential author born in 1822, might be considered an exception because of his use of OK in "The Brick Moon," published in 1870–71 and discussed here in Chapter 7. But in that story OK is strictly limited to a long-distance means of communication, not employed in conversation or narrative.)

Emily Dickinson, Louisa May Alcott, Horatio Alger, Mark Twain, Bret Harte, William Dean Howells, and Henry Adams were born in the 1830s and would have had the opportunity to encounter OK from their childhood. Nevertheless, they avoided OK. It doesn't appear even in the dialect humor of Twain and Harte.

Born later than OK were Ambrose Bierce, Joel Chandler Harris, Sarah Orne Jewett, James Whitcomb Riley, Kate Chopin, Mary E. Wilkins Freeman, Charlotte Perkins Gilman, Edith Wharton, Stephen Crane, Upton Sinclair—the list goes on and on. It is possible that an occasional OK lurks on an obscure page by one of those writers, but it is unquestionable that OK is about as plentiful in their writing as hens' teeth.

There are two qualifications to that statement that only serve to confirm the deliberate avoidance of OK by literary writers. Henry David Thoreau and Louisa May Alcott both have single instances of OK—and both were removed in revision.

Thoreau's Tailoress

Thoreau was the first. In 1850 he wrote in his journal,

> When I ask for a garment of a particular form, my tailoress
> tells me gravely, "They do not make them so now," and I find
> it difficult to get made what I want, simply because she cannot
> believe that I mean what I say: it surpasses her credulity. Prop-
> erly speaking, my style is as fashionable as theirs. "They do not
> make them so now," as if she quoted the Fates! I am for a
> moment absorbed in thought, thinking, wondering who *they*
> are, where *they* live. It is some Oak Hall, O call, O.K., all cor-
> rect establishment which she knows but I do not. Oliver
> Cromwell. I emphasize and in imagination italicize each word
> separately of that sentence to come at the meaning of it.

Oak Hall was a "clothier's establishment," to use a phrase current then, and Thoreau is at his most playful as he turns the name
into OK. But apparently he considered it too irrelevant, too dis-
tracting from his message to allow in print. The passage from the
journal appears in *Walden,* published in 1854, with considerable
revision:

> When I ask for a garment of a particular form, my tailoress
> tells me gravely, "They do not make them so now," not empha-
> sizing the "They" at all, as if she quoted an authority as imper-
> sonal as the Fates, and I find it difficult to get made what I
> want, simply because she cannot believe that I mean what I
> say, that I am so rash. When I hear this oracular sentence, I am
> for a moment absorbed in thought, emphasizing to myself
> each word separately that I may come at the meaning of it,
> that I may find out by what degree of consanguinity *They* are
> related to *me*, and what authority they may have in an affair

which affects me so nearly; and, finally, I am inclined to answer
her with equal mystery, and without any more emphasis of the
"they"—"It is true, they did not make them so recently, but
they do now."

Thoreau was hardly a man to insist on gentility, or to avoid
playing with language, but evidently he thought OK unsuited to
his purpose.

Alcott's Omitted Okay

The other exception—and subsequent omission—comes in the
hugely successful and still well-known novel *Little Women* by Louisa
May Alcott. If there were an annual prize for literary use of
OK, in 1869 it would have been hers by default. It isn't absolutely
the first literary instance of OK, but it's surprisingly modern,
including the spelling *okay*. In fact, it is the first known instance of
that four-letter spelling.

Little Women is the story of the spirited March sisters of Con-
cord, Massachusetts. The most refined and artistic of the four sisters is Amy, who uses the more refined spelling *okay* in a letter
from Heidelberg, Germany, to her mother in Massachusetts while
on a tour of Europe with her aunt, uncle, and cousin. Amy explains
why she'll be ready to accept the English gentleman Fred Vaughn's
proposal of marriage if it comes:

> I've made up my mind, and if Fred asks me, I shall accept him,
> though I'm not madly in love. I like him, and we get on com-
> fortably together. He is handsome, young, clever enough, and
> very rich—ever so much richer than the Laurences. . . .
>
>   I may be mercenary, but I hate poverty, and don't mean to
> bear it a minute longer than I can help. One of us must marry

well. Meg didn't, Jo won't, Beth can't yet, so I shall, and make everything okay all round. I wouldn't marry a man I hated or despised. You may be sure of that, and though Fred is not my model hero, he does very well, and in time I should get fond enough of him if he was very fond of me, and let me do just as I liked. So I've been turning the matter over in my mind the last week, for it was impossible to help seeing that Fred liked me. . . .

Of course this is all very private, but I wished you to know what was going on. Don't be anxious about me, remember I am your "prudent Amy," and be sure I will do nothing rashly. Send me as much advice as you like. I'll use it if I can. I wish I could see you for a good talk, Marmee. Love and trust me.

This passage comes in the second volume of *Little Women*, which Alcott wrote rapidly, early in 1869, in response to the commercial success of the first volume, published the year before. It is likely that she put *okay* in Amy's letter without giving it a second thought. Alcott's characters are not above using slang and colloquialisms.

Little Women was revised and refined for an 1880 edition. It's not clear whether Alcott or her publisher made the changes, but they made the book noticeably more prim and proper, removing slang and regionalisms. Here is the central part of the passage involving *okay* in its 1880 version:

, , , One of us must marry well; Meg didn't, Jo won't, Beth can't yet, so I shall, and make everything cozy all round. I wouldn't marry a man I hated or despised. You may be sure of that, and, though Fred is not my model hero, he does very well, and, in time, I should get fond enough of him if he was very fond of me, and let me do just as I liked. So I've been

turning the matter over in my mind the last week, for it was
impossible to help seeing that Fred liked me. . . .

The editing adds a sprinkling of commas throughout the passage but makes only one change in vocabulary: *cozy* for *okay*. So
much for what a fashionable young woman might actually have
said or written to her mother.

Amy says earlier to her sisters: "You laugh at me when I say I
want to be a lady, but I mean a true gentlewoman in mind and
manners, and I try to do it as far as I know how. I can't explain
exactly, but I want to be above the little meannesses and follies and
faults that spoil so many women." Perhaps it is the mark of a gentlewoman to use the spelling *okay* rather than the more obtrusive
OK. Incidentally, at the end, Amy doesn't take up with Fred after
all, but rather marries the *Little Women's* childhood friend Laurie.

Ladies' Slang

Clues about the attitude toward OK among nineteenth-century
polite company may be found in *The Ladies' Repository*, a monthly
"devoted to literature, arts, and religion." An 1874 article on Americanisms quotes a "bilious Englishman": "certain common vulgar-
isms he regards as canonical and universal; for instance, 'O. K.'"
Two years later, Rev. J. W. M'Cormick remarks in an article called
"Talkers and Talking":

> In the slang dialect every thing is exaggerated. It never rains
> but it pours. Nothing is simply nice or desirable. It is "awful
> nice" or "O. K." or "bully."

Vulgarism, slang . . . not quite suited to a young lady of fashion, perhaps.

In the Rough

But OK is not totally absent from fiction of the nineteenth century, if we look far enough. When OK does appear in the writing of lesser-known authors, it is mostly in dialogue by lower-class or rustic characters, indicating that it was recognized as slang, and that, outside of business uses, it belonged to spoken rather than written discourse. Perhaps the spelling OK for *all correct* implied its use by illiterates. To follow OK through nineteenth-century literature is to take a romp in the backwoods.

Neither low class nor illiteracy would have prevented its use by Mark Twain, for example in the character of Huckleberry Finn, or by Bret Harte, but maybe for them too it was just too dumb a joke.

If they avoided OK, it couldn't have been for being obscene or blasphemous, because by no stretch of the imagination does OK belong to either of those categories. It must have been simply that they considered OK beneath notice. It wasn't very exciting, or picturesque, or emphatic. Run-of-the-mill writers put OK in the mouths of ignorant rustic stock characters; better writers found better, more colorful words.

There's a *Comedy of Fashion*, first performed in New York City in 1845, featuring an ignorant would-be snob, Mr. Snobson, who can't understand the bungled French of Mrs. Tiffany:

Mrs. Tiffany. (pointing to a chair with great dignity) Sassoyez vow, Monsur Snobson.
Snobson. I wonder what she's driving at? I aint up to the fashionable lingo yet! (*aside*) Eh? what? Speak a little louder, Marm?
Mrs. Tiffany. What ignorance! (*aside*)
Mr. Tiffany. I presume Mrs. Tiffany means that you are to take a seat.

Snobson. Ex-actly—very obliging of her—so I will. (*sits*) No cer-
emony amonst friends, you know—and likely to be nearer—
you understand? *O. K.,* all correct. How is Seraphina?
Mrs. Tiffany. Miss Tiffany is not visible this morning.

In 1858 *The Reformed Gambler*, "the history of the later years of
the life of Jonathan H. Green the Reformed Gambler," tells of a
steamboat on the Ohio River that took aboard from the "sucker
state," Illinois, "a party of men who bade fair, from appearance, to
be a party not only susceptible of being fleeced, but one that would
pay for the pains." The boat's clerk questions their captain's request
to be registered under a false name.

"Oh, all is O.K.!" replied the sucker captain, placing his fingers upon his nose. "I am a *captain* at present. Did you not see
my men? Have I not paid their passages for the deck? That's
all!"—finishing the sentence by a request for the clerk, Rob-
erts, and Captain Harris to keep "dark."

There is *The Arkansas Traveller's Songster*: "Containing the celebrated story of the Arkansas traveler, with the music for violin or
piano. And also an extensive and choice collection of new and popular
comic and sentimental songs," published in New York City during the
Civil War. The songs include a parody on "Mother, I've Come Home
to Die," "an original conglomeration of titles," with the chorus:

"Call me pet names," "Annie Lisle,"
"A bully boy with a glass eye";
"Oh, let her rip! she's all O. K."—
"Dear mother, I've come home to die."

Unfortunately, the source of the quotation in the third line
remains elusive.

We can find another OK in *The Book of Humour, Wit and Wisdom*, published in Boston in 1874. Here is the complete story of "A Thoughtful Husband":

> The following story is told:—"I say, Cap'n!" cried a little keen-eyed man, as he landed from a steamer at Natchez, "I say, Cap'n, these here aren't all. I have left somethin' on board, that's a fact." "Them's all the plunder you brought on board, anyhow," answered the captain. "Wal, I see now; I grant it's O.K. accordin' to list; four boxes, three chests, two band-boxes, and portmanty; two hams, one part-cut, three ropes of inyens, and a tea-kettle. But see, Cap'n, I'm dubersome; I feel there's somethin' short, tho' I've counted um nine times over, and never took my eyes off um while on board; there's somethin' not right, somehow." "Wal, stranger, time's up; thems all I knows on; so just fetch your wife and five children out of the cabin, cos I'm off." "Thems um! Darn it, thems um! I know'd I'd forgot somethin'!"

In 1874 Lillie Devereux Blake's *Fettered for Life; or, Lord and Master. A Story of Today* was published in New York City. An abusive husband has this conversation with his intimidated wife when he stumbles into his house at five in the morning:

> "Has every thing gone right, John?" she asked.
>
> "Yes, of course, the Judge is elected by a big majority. It's been hard work; but it's all O. K. now."
>
> "I didn't mean that; but—but," looking at him with an awful horror in her questioning eyes—"was there any row? any body hurt?"
>
> The man drew his black brows together and turned on her fiercely.

The Wild West

In works of fiction, the vocabulary of rustic denizens of the Wild West at least now and then included OK. "A Singular Case," a story of a search for a mine in the West published in 1883 in *The Living Age*, features extensive dialogue in dialect by old-timer Bill.

> "Nary time," replied Bill, "an' thet's the curos part o' it—not so curos neither, wen ye think it over. This yer Burnfield must ha' gone inter the Smoky Hill in '57 at least. At thet time—but, demme, I allus git confused like wen I think back so fur—anyhow, I know Granite hedn't no more'n six or eight houses then; an' men wur all-fired skerce yer them days, an' often came an' went without tellin' whur they come from or whur they was goin'. It wurn't healthy to be too inquisitive, an' ax too many questions. It wur like thet wen I first remember Granite, an' thet wur—ah—nigh onto fourteen year ago. Nobody axed me whur I come from; mebbe I didn't know—an' I'm certing I didn't care."

This led later to:

> "Wal," said Bill, with considerable satisfaction, "that fixes us all O.K."

In the 1890s, a number of stories in *Overland Monthly* included rustic characters whose vocabulary included OK. Readers of "A Night Ride in Apache Land" by W. R. Rowe in an 1892 issue were treated to this dialogue:

> "Be sure and cinch 'em well, boys—we can't stop to tighten 'em after we git started."
> "Ay, ay, yer kin bet on us, Jack."
> "Are yer all O. K.?"
> "You bet."

"Then head fer the Baldy Mountain an' if ever you spurred, spur this night."

In 1895 another *Overland Monthly* story, "Tim Slather's Ride," by Granville P. Hurst, has this comment on the eponymous hero by a "Mizzoorah" farmer:

"Mighty nice young fellow," said farmer Hawley to his daughter, Bessie. "Gads about too much, an' don't seem to take natchelly to farm work. But I guess he'll settle down stiddy when he gits married. 'Taint every young man as has sich prospects as him. Ole man Slathers'll make 'im partner, if he'll go to work an' quit runnin' 'round to every blame place whur he has a chance o' showin' off his ridin'. Tim's all O. K. An', Bessie," added Mr. Hawley, lowering his voice and speaking slowly, as if in doubt just how, or how far, to proceed, "I sometimes kinder wish—'at you—an' him"—and overcome with the ardor or magnitude of his wish, Mr. Hawley stuck fast on the words and came to a full stop.

In 1899, "Sweet Evalina" by Elwyn Irving Hoffman in *Overland Monthly* features a rustic bachelor farmer and storyteller who recalls his long-ago sweetheart, assuring his educated interlocutor that he doesn't mind telling about it:

Clark laughed reassuringly. "O, that's all O K," he said; "it happened a long time ago, an' don't hurt me none now. A feller gits over things like that, you know, an' I'd jest as soon tell you about her as not; only, there ain't nothin' to tell."

In "How the Overalls Won: A Football Tale" by Carroll Carrington in a 1900 issue of the *Overland Monthly*, the cultivated narrator, an easterner, puts on a "drawl" in a mining camp, and "I was easily accepted for the ignoramus I wished them to think me."

Driscol finally cleared his throat.

"Do you mean to say, you idiot, that you're going to bring a foot-ball team up here tomorrow?" he demanded, indignantly.

"To-morrer," I repeated affably. "Yep. Couldn't get 'em here any sooner. Anyhow we couldn't play on Sunday, and I didn't get a chanst to tell the boys about you folks bein' up here practicin' until only a couple o' days or so ago. But they'll get here tomorrer all right, O. K., without fail, sure pop. Don't you worry."

At a somewhat higher literary level, Hamlin Garland, a regional writer of the Midwest and West still held in some esteem nowadays, doesn't entirely shun OK in the narrative of his adventures in the Klondike gold rush, *The Trail of the Goldseekers*, published in 1899. Toward the end of the book he is returning to his Wisconsin home by train, solicitous of his beloved horse Ladrone, who is traveling by another train.

Leaving him a tub of water, I bade him good-by once more and started him for Helena, five hundred miles away.

At Missoula, the following evening, I rushed into the ticket office and shouted, "Where is '54'?"

The clerk knew me and smilingly extended his hand.

"How de do? She has just pulled out. The horse is all O K. We gave him fresh water and feed."

OK Takes a Turn

So OK continued in that manner throughout the nineteenth century, known to writers and used by them occasionally, but not often, in dialogue involving pretentious, lowlife, or rustic characters. But as the nineteenth century turned into the twentieth, OK

took a turn too. It was a subtle turn, because it still involved unso-
phisticated characters, but OK in its quiet way began to take on a
role in humor and satire. This wasn't new for OK; after all, it began
as a joke, and for much of the nineteenth century it inspired
humorous interpretations of the initials OK. But this time it was
different. OK took on a secondary role, moving to the background
as a natural accompaniment to the humor rather than the focus of
it. We see this in three early twentieth-century writers: George
Ade, Ring Lardner, and Sinclair Lewis. Perhaps it is no coincidence that all were from the Midwest rather than the East Coast.

Aided by Ade

George Ade was from Indiana and had his first success writing for
Chicago newspapers. He was noted for incorporating smart everyday slang in his stories, and that included OK.

Ade helped make OK cool. Until Ade came along, OK was the
language of the uncouth, but his satirical Fables in Slang series
includes OK in the vocabulary of a knowing narrator. From *More
Fables* (1900), his second collection, OK appears in "The Fable of
the Regular Customer and the Copper-Lined Entertainer," about
a Country Customer who is wined and dined past remembrance
by a designated employee of a wholesale concern, thereby ensuring
the customer's business:

> The Head of the Concern put his O.K. on a Voucher for
> $43.66, and it occurred to him that Stereopticon Lectures
> seemed to be Advancing, but he asked no Questions.

Several more OKs found their way into Ade's next collection of
modern fables, *People You Know* (1903). This is from "The Search for
the Right House and How Mrs. Jump Had Her Annual Attack":

Mother was looking for a House that had twice as many Clos-
ets as Rooms and a Southern Exposure on all four sides.

She had conned herself into the Belief that some day she
would run down a Queen Anne Shack that would be O.K. in
all Particulars.

Also from *People You Know*, "The Summer Vacation That Was
Too Good to Last":

It was a lovely Time-Table that he had mapped out. He sub-
mitted it to Pet before she went away and she put her O.K. on
it, even though her Heart ached for him.

Ade's 1904 fable "The Night-Watch and the Would-be Something Awful," about "a full-sized Girl named Florine whose Folks
kept close Tab on her," ends with an OK moral:

Florine would have remained a Dead Card if she had not gone
on a Visit to a neighboring City where she bumped into the
Town Trifler. He had a Way of proposing to every Girl the first
time he met her. It always seemed to him such a cordial Send-
Off for a budding Friendship. Usually the Girl asked for Time
and then the two of them would Fiddle around and Fuss and
Make Up and finally send back all the Letters and that would be
the Finish. Florine fooled the foxy Philander. The Moment he
came at her with the Marriage Talk she took a firm Hold and
said, "You're on! Get your License to-morrow morning. Then
cut all the Telegraph Wires and burn the Railroad Bridges."

They were Married, and, strange as it may appear, Mother
immediately resigned her Job as Policeman and said: "Thank goodness, I've got you Married Off! Now you can do as you please."

When Florine found that she could do as she pleased she
discovered that there wasn't very much of anything to do

except Settle Down. After about seven Chafing-Dish Parties she expended her whole Stock of pent-up Ginger and now she is just as Quiet as the rest of us.

   MORAL: Any System is O.K. if it finally Works Out.

You Know Me, Al

What Ade did for OK was significant, but it pales in comparison with the contribution of Ring Lardner, another newspaperman and humorist from Chicago. He adopted the persona of a naive, self-important, semiliterate baseball player, a pitcher who is signed by the Chicago White Sox and who writes to a friend back home about big-league baseball. The serialized columns were collected in *You Know Me Al: A Busher's Letters Home*, published in 1916. The letters abound with OK, some forty-two instances according to Google Books. Here the fictional Jack Keefe tells of negotiating a contract with the (real) White Sox owner, Charles Comiskey:

> We kidded each other back and forth like that a while and then he says You better go out and get the air and come back when you feel better. I says I feel O.K. now and I want to sign a contract because I have got to get back to Bedford.

Later, Jack ponders a marital problem, using four OKs:

CHICAGO, ILLINOIS, JANUERY 31.

AL: Allen is going to take Marie with him on the training trip to California and of course Florrie [Jack's new wife] has been at me to take her along. I told her postivly that she can't go. I can't afford no stunt like that but still I am up against it to know what to do with her while we are on the trip because Marie won't be here to stay with her. I don't like to leave her here all alone but they is nothing to it Al I can't afford to take her along. She says I don't see why you can't take me if Allen takes Marie. And I says That stuff is all O.K. for Allen because him and Marie has been grafting off of us all winter. And then she gets mad and tells me I should not ought to say her sister was no grafter. I did not mean nothing like that Al but you don't never know when a woman is going to take offense. If our furniture was down in Bedford everything would be all O.K. because I could leave her there and I would feel all O.K. because I would know that you and Bertha would see that she was getting along O.K. But they would not be no sense in sending her down to a house that has not no furniture in it. I wish I knowed somewheres where she could visit Al. I would be willing to pay her bord even.

WELL AL ENOUGH FOR THIS TIME.
YOUR OLD PAL, JACK.

Lardner's famous 1915 short story "Alibi Ike," about another baseball player who "never pulled a play, good or bad, on or off the field, without apologizin' for it," includes more examples:

"You got a swell girl, Ike," I says.

"She's a peach," says Smitty.

"Well, I guess she's O. K.," says Ike. "I don't know much about girls."

"Didn't you never run round with 'em?" I says.

"Oh, yes, plenty of 'em," says Ike. "But I never seen none I'd fall for."

"That is, till you seen this one," says Carey.

"Well," says Ike, "this one's O. K., but I wasn't thinkin' about gettin' married yet a wile."

Lardner's 1920 novel *The Big Town* is about a couple from South Bend, Indiana, who inherit money and move to New York City with the wife's sister. The wife looks for an apartment, and the husband, who is the narrator, comments:

> Well, they showed me over the whole joint and it did look O.K., but not $4,000 worth. The best thing in the place was a half full bottle of rye in the kitchen that the cripple hadn't gone south with. I did.

A famous aviator invites him to take a ride:

> Well, the four of us set there and talked about this and that, and Codd said he hadn't had time to get his machine put together yet, but when he had her fixed and tested her a few times he would take me up for a ride.
>
>   "You got the wrong number," I says. "I don't feel flighty."
>
>   "Oh, I'd just love it!" said Kate.
>
>   "Well," says Codd, "you ain't barred. But I don't want to have no passengers along till I'm sure she's working O.K."

The language is pointedly nonstandard, but here and elsewhere in Lardner's writing OK is put to its modern everyday uses. It is no longer a funny abbreviation but a breezy way of indicating that matters are all right.

Ring Lardner's example was catching. In 1921 Donald Ogden Stewart, another humorist and later a member of the witty Algonquin Round Table, wrote *A Parody Outline of History*, with each chapter in the style of a noted contemporary author, among them Edith Wharton, F. Scott Fitzgerald, Eugene O'Neill, and Sinclair Lewis. Chapter 5 is "The Spirit of '75: Letters of a Minute Man in the Manner of Ring Lardner." Here's that Minute Man:

Friend Ethen—

> Well Ethen you will be surprised O. K. to hear I & the
> wife took a little trip down to Boston last wk. to a T.
> party & I guess you are thinking we will be getting the
> swelt hed over being ast to a T. party. In Boston.

And later:

> After supper I & her was walking a round giving the town the
> double O when we seen that Fanny Ewell Hall was all lit up like
> Charley Davis on Sat. night & I says to Prudence lets go inside I
> think its free and she says I bet you knowed it was free al right
> befor you ast me & sure enough it was free only I hadnt knowed
> it before only I guess that Prudence knows that when I say a
> thing it is generally O. K.

And finally, on a historical occasion:

> Well the other night I and Prudence was sound asleep when I
> heard some body banging at the frt. door & I stuck my head
> out the up stares window & I says who are you & he says I am
> Paul Revear & I says well this is a h—ll of a time to be wakeing
> a peaceful man out of their bed what do you want & he says
> the Brittish are comeing & I says o are they well this is the 19 of
> April not the 1st & I was going down stares to plank him 1 but
> he had rode away tow wards Lexington before I had a chanct &
> as it turned out after words the joke was on me O. K.

Sinclair Lewis: OK Businessmen

George Ade and Ring Lardner were out-and-out humorists. Sinclair Lewis, though a satirist, wasn't, so his use of OK in dialogue
reflects its acceptance as a normal component of American con-

versation, at least in the business world he satirizes. Here's a passage from his 1914 novel, *Our Mr. Wrenn: The Romantic Adventures of a Gentle Man*:

> That same afternoon the manager enthusiastically O. K.'d the plan. To enthusiastically-O. K. is an office technology for saying, gloomily, "Well, I don't suppose it 'd hurt to try it, anyway, but for the love of Mike be careful, and let me see any letters you send out."
>
> So Mr. Wrenn dictated a letter to each of their Southern merchants, sending him a Dixieland Ink-well and inquiring about the crops. He had a stenographer, an efficient intolerant young woman who wrote down his halting words as though they were examples of bad English she wanted to show her friends, and waited for the next word with cynical amusement.

And from Lewis's 1920 novel *Main Street*:

> Despite Aunt Bessie's nagging the Kennicotts rarely attended church. The doctor asserted, "Sure, religion is a fine influence—got to have it to keep the lower classes in order—fact, it's the only thing that appeals to a lot of those fellows and makes 'em respect the rights of property. And I guess this theology is O.K.; lot of wise old coots figured it all out, and they knew more about it than we do."

Lewis's 1922 satire *Babbitt* likewise has examples of OK in dialogue. Here is one:

> This fellow Graff you got working for you, he leases me a house. I was in yesterday and signs the lease, all O.K., and he was to get the owner's signature and mail me the lease last night.

Later a speaker addresses the Boosters' Club:

> Some of you may feel that it's out of place here to talk on a
> strictly highbrow and artistic subject, but I want to come out
> flatfooted and ask you boys to O.K. the proposition of a Sym-
> phony Orchestra for Zenith. Now, where a lot of you make
> your mistake is in assuming that if you don't like classical
> music and all that junk, you ought to oppose it.

These authors who used OK in modern ways may not have insti-
gated the change from the old funny abbreviation, but they
reflected it. By the time the twentieth century was well under
way, OK had moved from the fringe of American English to the
center.

OKLAHOMA
IS OK

WAIT A MINUTE. WHAT ABOUT OKLAHOMA?

Oklahoma is OK, no doubt about it. It's not just the postal abbreviation; it's even proclaimed on license plates and T-shirts, and it's the inspiration for business names in Oklahoma, everything from OK Paintless Dent Repairs in Duncan to OK Goat Coop, a goat farm in Tulsa.

And yet Oklahoma is a Johnny-come-lately to the world of OK. It could have played a role in the nineteenth- or early twentieth-century development of OK, but it was only in the mid-twentieth century when the connection between Oklahoma and OK became prominent.

The connection could have begun as long ago as 1866, when the name *Oklahoma* was proposed for the newly legislated Indian

Territory that was the predecessor of the state. Chief Allen Wright of the Choctaw Indians suggested *Oklahoma,* literally "red people," used in Choctaw to designate all Native Americans. This became the name of the territory in 1890 and remained the name when Oklahoma attained statehood in 1907. But it wasn't abbreviated OK.

The distinctive word associated with Oklahoma in its early days was not OK but *sooner.* When the federal government opened the "Unassigned Lands" of Indian Territory with a land run across the territorial border at noon on April 22, 1889, the settlers who rushed in found that certain others had managed to arrive there sooner to stake their claims. Among the "sooners" were surveyors, railroad men, and officers of the law, who had legitimate reasons for being in the territory early and who took the opportunity to stake out the best 160-acre plots for themselves. A somewhat grudging admiration for their initiative led to Oklahoma eventually being labeled the Sooner State, even by Oklahomans. Better, perhaps, than the Hoosier State for Indiana, or the Sucker State for Illinois. For better or worse, it had nothing to do with OK.

Nor did the state's motto, adopted by the Territorial Legislative Assembly in 1893. To this day Oklahoma's Great Seal bears the legend "Labor Omnia Vincit," not from an Indian language or from English but from the poet Virgil's classical Latin, "Labor Conquers All."

The state flag likewise makes no use of OK. Its first version was simply a white star with the number 46 (for the forty-sixth state) on a red background. The next and current flag has an Indian motif, a warrior's shield crossed by a peace pipe, on a blue background with the name of the state beneath. No abbreviation.

And for many years the official postal abbreviation, as well as the one used in newspapers, was the four-letter *Okla.*

It took many years, and a song and ZIP code, to bring Oklahoma and OK together.

The song, of course, is from the 1943 musical *Oklahoma!* Written by Oscar Hammerstein II in his first collaboration with composer Richard Rodgers, the song was such a hit that it became the title of the musical, displacing the original *Away We Go!* The musical was based on a 1931 play by Jean Riggs, *Green Grow the Rushes*, but that play has nary an OK.

It's not as if OK permeates the musical, however. It's absent until the very end. But there it holds a strategic place, repeated three times at the end of the refrain of the final song. It's the very last word as the curtain comes down and the audience begins to applaud. Here is that ending, with the spelling used in Oklahoma Statutes Title 25, Chapter 3, Section 94.3, when "Oklahoma!" was adopted as the official state song in 1953:

> . . . We know we belong to the land
> And the land we belong to is grand!
> And when we say—Yeeow! A-yip-i-o-ee ay!
> We're only sayin' You're doin' fine, Oklahoma!
> Oklahoma—O.K.

That popular musical was the first big step in making OK at home in Oklahoma, and it prepared the way for the next. In 1963 the U.S. Post Office introduced ZIP codes and with them two-letter abbreviations for each state. What else could stand for Oklahoma besides OK? Even the distinctive practice of capitalizing both letters of the abbreviation encouraged the connection. Thus Oklahoma was transformed from *Okla.* to OK.

And that, in turn, evidently was the inspiration for the legend on the state license plate, "Oklahoma Is OK," first issued in 1967. It was followed in 1987 by the shorter declaration "Oklahoma OK!"

Today, making use of the abbreviation, there are businesses like OK Handyman and OK Alliance for Manufacturing Excellence, in Tulsa, and in Oklahoma City you'll find OK Experts LLC, a handyman service, and OK Nails, a beauty shop. But there really aren't that many Oklahoma businesses with OK in their names. A comedian can draw a laugh at the slogan "Oklahoma is OK." And even if it's not a joke, as we have noted in a previous chapter, OK just doesn't imply much enthusiasm.

So Oklahoma could have played a starring role in the history of OK. Instead, it's just OK.

OKEY-DOKEY

BY THE EARLY TWENTIETH CENTURY, OK WAS NO LONGER
a joke. The letters *O* and *K* did not prompt memories of the misspelled *oll korrect*, nor did they stimulate alternative explanations.
In the nineteenth century, OK was recognized as a humorous
abbreviation, but in the twentieth, it was understood merely as an
arbitrary combination of letters of the alphabet.

The very look of OK underwent a change. In the nineteenth century, OK almost always appeared with periods, iden-
tifying it as an abbreviation. In the twentieth, however, the
periods increasingly were absent. And in the twentieth century,
more and more it was spelled *okay*, completely distancing it
from any abbreviation and transforming it into an ordinary
word.

The meaning of OK was simplified in the twentieth century too. Almost from the date of its birth, in the nineteenth century the abbreviation OK was subject to reinterpretation, beginning with Old Kinderhook and continuing with numerous humorous inventions, as well as the names of clubs. As the twentieth century got under way, those alternatives faded, leaving OK for the most part with the plain, sober definition "all right."

Gaining familiarity rather than passion, OK also gained the abbreviation *oke* in the 1920s, and *kay* or just plain *k*, both in writing (nowadays including text messages and e-mail) and speaking.

Along with the draining of humor from OK came the draining of enthusiasm, or indeed of any emotion. In 1840 the OK Clubs could inspire voters to support Old Kinderhook for reelection. The clubs formed later in the nineteenth century, from the Harvard OK on down, likewise kept OK spirited. In occasional literary use, OK often colorfully evoked the voice of a decidedly backwoods character. But by the early twentieth century, OK had become value-neutral. It remained affirmative, but it imparted no attributes, admirable or otherwise, as it remains today. When a friend nowadays asks "What do you think of my garden?" to answer "OK" is likely to make the respondent the target of a flowerpot. You'd better use a value word like *wonderful* or *perfect*. Even *terrible* shows more emotional involvement than OK.

So OK no longer was a joke or a showstopper. In the nineteenth century, OK stood out, but in the twentieth, OK was just OK.

To make OK funny in the twentieth century, or to give it emphasis, it needed a twist. And the Roaring Twenties came up with it—several twists, in fact. Beginning in the 1920s we find such twists as *okey-dokey* and *oke-doke*, leading up to the *okely-dokely* now used by cartoon character Ned Flanders on the television show *The Simpsons*.

The rise of *okey-dokey* and its relatives took away the pressure on OK to be funny. Once *okey-dokey* made its appearance, any vestige of humor associated with OK fled to its polysyllabic progeny, leaving OK free of all remaining traces of playfulness. We are inclined to smile when we hear *okey-dokey*; we hear plain OK with a straight face. The expression born as a blatant joke a century earlier had now become a sober workhorse, ready to undertake ventures in pragmatics and psychology in the postwar years.

Here are some examples of the new twists on old OK. From a 1924 issue of George Jean Nathan and H. L. Mencken's *American Mercury*:

> Papa Satan, he said, Okey doke! Here we go round and round the old-time mulberry bush! When the woman say no, she really mean yes!

From an article on contemporary slang in the *Philadelphia Inquirer* of June 16, 1929:

> As in non-collegiate circles, the ponderous O. K. has given way to the snappier "oke." There is a sonorous note about this expression, the compiler says, which has made its vogue immense. Among elite slangsters, in fact, it has almost completely ousted older expressions.

In 1934 a hearing before the U.S. Senate's Special Committee to Investigate the Munitions Industry elicited the testimony "that tying it up in this bill, it was all 'okey-dokey.'"

The "Notes and Comment" section of the *New Yorker* for February 23, 1935, offered a variant spelling:

> It's been quite a month. . . . A witness in a civil action in Seattle stopped the trial when he answered "Oakie-doke" to a question.

And the *Log*, the publication of the American Society of Marine Engineers, reported in 1935 from the heartland:

> SOUTH DAKOTA.—Everything is okey-doke (excuse it, please) as the state is slopping around in the mud in a way it hasn't done in several years. It's such a striking change from last year.

It shows up in *Streamline for Health* by Philip Bovier Hawk, a diet book published by Harper & Brothers in 1935:

> Simply subtract 450 calories from your regular food intake and everything will be okey dokey.

William Faulkner's novel about flying, *Pylon*, published in 1935, includes among its characters Jiggs, a mechanic:

> "Okey doke," Jiggs said. The aeroplane waddled out and onto the runway and turned and stopped.

In the *New Yorker* in 1936, humorist James Thurber was inspired to respond with *okie-dokie* to a book titled *Wake Up and Live!*:

> Now Mrs. Dorothea Brande has written a book and Simon & Schuster have published it, with the grim purpose in mind of getting me and all the other woolgatherers mentally organized so that, in a world which is going to pieces, we can be right up on our toes. . . . I don't want a copy of the book; in fact, I don't need one. I have got the gist of the idea of "Wake Up and Live!" from reading an advertisement for it in the Sunday Times book section. The writer of the ad said that Mrs. Brande in her inspirational volume suggests "twelve specific disciplines," and he names these, in abbreviated form. I'll take

them up in order and show why it is no use for Mrs. Brande to try to save me if these disciplines are all she has to offer:

. . .

"9. Eliminate the phrases 'I mean' and "As a matter of fact' from your conversation."

Okie-dokie.

"10. Plan to live two hours a day according to a rigid time schedule."

Well, I usually wake up at nine in the morning and lie there till eleven.

The phrase was associated with the rustic language of farmers in the 1938 Federal Writers' Project book *Delaware: A Guide to the First State.*

The Delaware section of US 13 runs more than one-half the length of the so-called Delmarva Peninsula, the low-lying and water-bound region east of Chesapeake Bay that contains the State of Delaware and the Eastern Shores of Maryland and Virginia.

Bordered by few famous buildings and no battlefields or natural wonders but by a countryside of comfortable farmsteads, busy towns and villages, and numerous vistas of quiet beauty, the route is notable for the successive differences and contrasts, great and small, in the aspect of the country and in the life of the people. Within 25 miles there may be differences in terrain, forestation, style or material of old houses, political color, crops and farming methods, tempo of living, accent and expression of speech. A farmer who lives in the southern part of the State and drives a truck-load of vegetables to Wilmington every week, may say "oakie-doke" in one breath and then speak of "housen" for houses, or of a chicken too long killed as "dainty."

Joe Falls, in the 1977 book *50 Years of Sports Writing (and I Still Can't Tell the Difference Between a Slider and a Curve)*, indicates one of the consequences of choosing *okey-dokey*: In a serious statement, it doesn't inspire as much confidence as plain OK.

> Another time we were flying to Kansas City on a four-engine plane when one of the engines conked out. The pilot told us he had to "feather" it because it was giving him some trouble. No problem, though, he said. He would just detour to Chicago and everything would be okey-dokey. That's what he said. Okey-dokey.
>
> As I walked down the aisle, I could feel my feet pressing into the floor. Okey-dokey, my butt.

Jump ahead to August 1994 and the *Misc. Newsletter*, a report on popular culture in Seattle and beyond by Clark Humphrey:

> PR LINE OF THE WEEK (postcard to a band's mailing list): "This is a postcard to promote 'Running with Scissors' and to tell you things are going to be okie dokie. . . . The Scissors Manifesto: 1. Attending our shows and buying our CDs are the keys to 'okie dokie-ness.' 2. People who request our songs on the radio are okie dokie. 3. Actually, sex is much better than 'okie dokie-ness' but no one will pay us for sex. 4. It would be really great if young people had a reason to feel better than just okie dokie. 5. Foul tasting, over-hyped beverages do not make you feel okie dokie . . . Not affiliated with any patronizing multinational beverage company."

As OK did in certain nineteenth-century contexts, *okey-dokey* in recent times can suggest lack of education, or more positively, simplicity of character. In *And the Angels Laughed: 101 Anecdotes and Devotionals* (2007), Barbara Eubanks tells of a lady who came down the aisle and told the pastor she wanted to be saved. He asked her if she wanted to talk to the Lord about it.

> She replied, "I done did."
> "Well, what did he say?" prodded the pastor.
> "He said, 'Okey-dokey.'"
> I'm not sure what colloquial expressions the Lord uses, but I'm sure he speaks to people in terms they understand.

The playfulness of *okey-dokey* is evident when it turns up as the name for a recipe in *Fondue* by Lenny Rice and Brigid Callinan, published in 2007. The artichoke fondue "Okey-dokey Artichokey" is to be paired with Austrian grüner veltliner, which "has a crisp, peppery quality that makes it one of the only reliable artichoke-friendly wines we know."

Perhaps the name of the recipe was inspired by a children's book published four years earlier, *Okie-dokie, Artichokie!* by Grace Lin. That's the story of a new downstairs neighbor named Artichoke who bangs mysteriously on his ceiling, the protagonist's floor. "Hey, if I get too loud or something, you can just bang on the ceiling and let me know," says the protagonist, who happens to be a monkey. The downstairs neighbor is a giraffe, hence the inadvertent banging.

And there's a fictitious Okie-Dokie Corral in Houston, where the Cheetah Girls, a group of young African American singers in search of success, compete against their archrivals the Cash Money Girls in *Showdown at the Okie-Dokie* (2000), number 9 in the Cheetah Girls series, aimed at girls in grades four through six.

Like OK itself, *okey-dokey* has traveled around the world, or so we gather from Autumn Cornwell's 2007 novel *Carpe Diem,* narrated by an overachieving sixteen-year-old who backpacks in Southeast Asia with a relative. In Cambodia, she orders from Peppy Pete of Peppy Pete's Pizzeria:

"So, one large pizza with everything—okey-dokey! Extra peppy?"

"Peppy? Oh, no. Nothing remotely spicy or peppy for me."

"Okey-dokey!"

"Oh, and a bottle of Chianti," I said, but added hurriedly: "For my grandma."

"Okey-dokey smokey!" And he waddled off.

Of all present-day users of expanded versions of OK, however, the most famous is a cartoon character. Ned Flanders, the Simpsons' utterly good-natured and devoutly Christian next-door neighbor, is noted for extending the two-syllable OK into the six-syllable *okely-dokely*. He stretches out other words too, as in two 1993 episodes:

Ned: Hi-di-ly-hey, Camper Bart! You ready for today's meeting?
Bart: You know-dilly know it, Neddy.
Ned: Okely-dokely!

Todd (Ned's son): We're not going to church today!
Ned: What? You give me one good reason.
Todd: It's Saturday.
Ned: Okely-dokeley-doo!

In a 1996 episode, Homer prompts Ned to say it:

Ned: Homer, ah . . . About those things you borrowed from me over the years, you know, the TV trays, the power sander, the downstairs bathtub . . . You gonna be needing those things in Cypress Creek?
Homer: Yes.
Ned: Oh. Uh . . .

Homer: Okely-dokely.
Ned: Okely-dokely.

By now, *okey-dokey* (and variants like *okely-dokely*) has long lost its freshness—hence its suitability for a not-so-cool character like Ned Flanders. For some, it's an annoyance. Slang expert Tom Dalzell, in *The Concise New Partridge Dictionary of Slang and Unconventional English* (2007), acknowledges that *okey-dokey* is "used for communicating agreement," but he can't resist grumbling that it is "an old-fashioned, affected, still popular perversion of OK."

The Old Okey-Doke

There's another not so comical meaning for *okey-doke*, one that presidential candidate Barack Obama used in speaking to a predominantly African American audience in Sumter, South Carolina, on January 23, 2008. He said, in part:

> The point is, part of what happens in Washington is folks will twist your words around, trying to pretend you said something you didn't say, trying to pretend you didn't say something you did. We know that game. But that's the kind of politics that we've got to change. . . .
>
> So don't be confused when you hear a whole bunch of this negative stuff. Those are the same old tricks. They're trying to bamboozle you. It's the same old okey-doke. Y'all know about okey-doke, right? It's the same old stuff.
>
> It's like if anybody gets one of these e-mails saying, "Obama is a Muslim." I've been a member of the same church for almost twenty years, praying to Jesus, with my Bible. Don't let people turn you around. Because they're just making stuff up.

That's what they do. They try to bamboozle you. Hoodwink you. Try to hoodwink you.

In case anyone didn't know that definition of *okey-doke*, candidate Obama was liberal with paraphrase: *tricks, same old stuff, bamboozle, hoodwink.* But the audience probably did, since that meaning of *okey-doke* is current in the African American community.

It goes back a while. The *Historical Dictionary of American Slang* has examples of this meaning as early as 1967. Researcher Ben Zimmer found *okey-doke* in a 1989 quotation from Spike Lee ("We got robbed, gypped, jerked around—they gave us the okey-doke") and from Ice Cube in the movie *Trespass* ("They're lying to you, K.J., laughing behind your back, got us going for the okey-doke").

And on a community forum website for Southport, Connecticut, in December 2008, "The Judge" posted this comment regarding the United Illuminating Company:

Right you are DPUC, it's the same old-same old, okey-dokey! One day these guys are on opposite fences, the next, they are sitting around at fundraisers together and scoffing down pigs in a blanket and cheap chablis.

MODERN OK
LITERATURE

AS WE HAVE SEEN IN CHAPTER 8, THE TURN OF THE TWENTIETH century brought a turn in the literary fortunes of OK. It never became the subject of a famous poem or the focus of a novel, but gradually it became OK to use OK in works of fiction without raising eyebrows. OK, sometimes in its more unobtrusive form *okay*, had lost its connotation of slang as it lost the memory of its silly origin. The literature of the past eighty years shows OK fully at home in its present-day uses.

For example, in Damon Runyon's short story "'Gentlemen, the King!'" published in *Collier's* magazine in 1931 and narrated in his distinctive pseudo-elegant gangster slang, *okay* plays a role:

So this lawyer takes me to the Ritz-Carlton hotel, and there he introduces me to a guy by the name of Count Saro, and the lawyer says he will okay anything Saro has to say to me 100 per cent, and then he immediately takes the wind as if he does not care to hear what Saro has to say. But I know this mouthpiece is not putting any proposition away as okay unless he knows it is pretty much okay, because he is a smart guy at his own dodge, and everything else, and has plenty of coco-nuts.

Henry Miller's 1934 *Tropic of Cancer,* in between the erotic passages that prevented its publication in the United States for a quarter century, includes some OKs:

Chicle, when it is gathered by *chicleros,* is O.K.

If he chooses to add martyrdom to his list of vices, let him— It's O.K. with me.

Zora Neale Hurston has an OK—just one—in her 1937 novel *Their Eyes Were Watching God*, about African American communities in Florida:

". . . Ah set in de kitchen one day and heard dat woman tell mah wife Ah'm too black fuh her. . . ."

. . .

"So she live offa our money and don't lak black folks, huh? O.K. we'll have her gone from here befo' two weeks is up. Ah'm goin' right off tuh all de men and drop rocks aginst her."

Ezra Pound, poet and pro-Fascist, had his own way with OK. In a 1938 letter from Rapallo, Italy, where he was living, to President Joseph Brewer of Olivet College declining the offer of a job and complaining about "the bestiality of curricula" at colleges, Pound comments:

Another question re/ dissociation of ideas ... The student shd SEE the actual producer. O.Kay. that is one side of the problem. I wonder if Ford [Madox Ford] has clearly cut it away from the other. . . . A country which does not FEED its best writers is a mere stinking dung heap.

William Faulkner was not above using an occasional OK, though it is scarce in his works. Here it is in his 1939 novella *The Old Man*:

"Take a drink or two. Give yourself time to feel it. If it's not good, no use in bringing it."

"O.K.," the deputy said.

John Steinbeck's *Grapes of Wrath* (1939), with its down-to-earth characters, has several dozen examples, including these:

"If you men want to sit here on your ass, O.K. I'm out getting men for Tulare County."

"O.K.," he said tiredly. "O.K. I shouldn', though. I know it."

Raymond Chandler, chronicler of the Los Angeles detective Philip Marlowe, preferred the spelling *okey* in his novels, including *The Big Sleep* (1939):

The purring voice from over in the shadows said: "Cut out the heavy menace, Art. This guy's in a jam. You run a garage, don't you?"

"Thanks," I said, and didn't look at him even then.

"Okey, okey," the man in the coveralls grumbled. He tucked his gun through a flap in his clothes and bit a knuckle, staring at me moodily over it.

And in *Farewell, My Lovely* (1940), after Marlowe has been drugged:

I sat up once more and planted my feet on the floor and stood up.

"Okey, Marlowe," I said between my teeth. "You're a tough guy. Six feet of iron man. One hundred and ninety pounds stripped and with your face washed. Hard muscles and no glass jaw. You can take it. You've been sapped down twice, had your throat choked and been beaten half silly on the jaw with a gun barrel. You've been shot full of hop and kept under it until you're as crazy as two waltzing mice. And what does all that amount to? Routine. Now let's see you do something really tough, like putting your pants on."

That spelling even comes through in a Portuguese translation:

"Okey, Marlowe," falei entre os dentes, "você é durão. . . ."

OK is found in the American hero's thoughts in Ernest Hemingway's *For Whom the Bell Tolls* (1940):

But you have behaved O.K.

But with the wire length you are using it's O.K., Robert Jordan thought.

Ralph Ellison's *Invisible Man* uses OK in a variety of ways:

"Okay, okay, take it easy," Halley said.

"Okay now," he said, "you can try to kid me but don't say I didn't wake you."

"Okay, brothers," the voice said, "let him pass."

"You're all right, boy. You're okay. You just be patient," said the voice.

OK shows up near the beginning of Ray Bradbury's *Fahrenheit 451* (1953):

"Sure, she'll be okay. We got all the mean stuff right in our suitcase here, it can't get at her now."

John Updike's 1959 *Rabbit, Run* includes OKs in dialogue:

"Yeah. O.K. I'll be right out."

"It's O.K., I'll pay," Rabbit says.

OK is scattered throughout Joseph Heller's World War II satire *Catch-22* (1961):

"Now, you go home and try it my way for a few months and see what happens. Okay?" "Okay," they said.

"Okay, fatmouth, out of the car," Chief Halfoat ordered.

Truman Capote's nonfiction novel *In Cold Blood* (1965) makes liberal use of OK in dialogue:

"O.K., sugar—whatever you say." Dick started the car.

"O.K. The first show was called 'The Man and the Challenge.' Channel 11."

He unlocked the door and said, "O.K. Let's go."

"Oh, they're together O.K. But driving a different car."

Kurt Vonnegut's World War II semi-memoir *Slaughterhouse-Five* (1969) uses OK too:

"You're all right, Sandy," I'll say to the dog. "You know that, Sandy? You're O.K."

And somewhere in there a nice man named Seymour Lawrence gave me a three-book contract, and I said, "O.K., the first of the three will be my famous book about Dresden."

Toni Morrison has OKs in *Song of Solomon* (1977):

"Okay," Freddie said, and threw up his hands. "Okay, laugh on. But they's a lot of strange things you don't know nothin about, boy."

and in *Beloved* (1987):

"Some?" he smiled. "Okay. Here's some. There's a carnival in town. Thursday, tomorrow, is for coloreds. . . ."

Celie, the narrator in Alice Walker's *The Color Purple* (1982), uses OK:

She giggle. Okay, she say. Nobody coming. Coast clear.

Bobbie Ann Mason's 1982 collection *Shiloh and Other Stories* (1982) includes OK in the title story:

"This is a pretty place. Your mama was right."
    "It's O.K.," says Norma Jean.

and in "The Rookers":

"Fluoride's O.K. It hardens the teeth."

These examples have been from the mid- and late twentieth century, but twenty-first-century writers continue to be comfortable with OK, sprinkling it more or less sparingly in their writing. Tom Wolfe's hefty 2004 novel of modern college life, *I Am Charlotte Simmons,* has a whole chapter titled "You Okay?" It's the one thing Charlotte's date at a fraternity formal in Washington, D.C., says to her when he takes her virginity in a drunken, sweaty episode in a hotel room. "Are you okay?" he asks, to which she murmurs "Mmnnnnh," wishing she could yell at him to stop. And then when he is finished:

"*Ahhhhhhhhhh*," he went, in a tone of immense satisfaction as he rolled over completely on his back. And then he said, "You okay?"

After that, Hoyt and the others who come and go in the hotel room ignore her except occasionally to wonder whether she is OK, when obviously she isn't. Then at the end of the chapter:

> Dreadfully hung over, a malady she had never experienced before, Charlotte had a brief coughing spasm in Maryland, and Hoyt said, "You okay?"
> She went, "Mmmnh," just so he would have a response, and she wouldn't say anything more. A couple of hours later, as he let her out in front of Little Yard, he said, "You okay?"
> She didn't so much as glance at him. She just walked away with her boat bag. He didn't ask twice.

And Stephen King doesn't shy from OK in his 2008 novel *Duma Key*, where it appears more than eighty times:

> "Okay," Ilse said at last.
> "Okay what?"
> "Okay, I'm worried."

> Things on Duma Key had been okay . . . then strange . . . then for a long time they'd been okay again. And now . . .

> "Edgar?" Jack touched my elbow. "Okay?"
> I was not okay, and wouldn't be okay for a long time again.

As these examples show, present-day writers employ OK without hesitation, particularly in dialogue, reflecting the present-day use of OK in actual everyday speech. Yet OK seems not to be as

frequent in fiction as it is in real life. It's just OK, not much of a
spicy ingredient for crackling dialogue.

There's a notable exception, however, that is saturated with
numerous OKs. It is Cormac McCarthy's *The Road* (2006), about
a man and his young son (about ten years old) wandering through
a postapocalyptic American landscape where the sun never shines
and every living thing has died except a few surviving and desper-
ate humans. Much of the book is dialogue, and you can scarcely
find a page of dialogue without OK. The dialogue itself is bleak,
stripped bare of quotation marks and some other punctuation
marks, like this, near the beginning of the book:

> Okay.
> Okay what?
> Just okay.
> Go to sleep.
> Okay.
> I'm going to blow out the lamp. Is that okay?
> Yes. That's okay.

In the middle:

> He looked down at the old man and he looked at the road. All
> right, he said. But then tomorrow we go on.
> The boy didnt answer.
> That's the best deal you're going to get.
> Okay.
> Okay means okay. It doesnt mean we negotiate another deal
> tomorrow.
> What's negotiate?
> It means talk about it some more and come up with some other
> deal. There is no other deal. This is it.

> Okay.
> Okay.

And near the end:

> Just dont give up. Okay?
> Okay.
> Okay.
> I'm really scared Papa.
> I know. But you'll be okay. You're going to be lucky. I know you are. I've got to stop talking. I'm going to start coughing again.
>   It's okay, Papa. You dont have to talk. It's okay.

McCarthy himself, like most of us, is a bona fide user of OK. Interviewed by Oprah Winfrey in 2007, he said, "You'd like for the people who would appreciate the book to read it. But as far as having many people reading it, so what? It's OK. Nothing wrong with it."

In a November 2009 discussion with a *Wall Street Journal* writer, McCarthy said, "A lot of the lines that are in there are verbatim conversations my son John and I had." Actual present-day conversations abound with OK, so that might account for its abundance in the book. And OK is only in the dialogue, not the third-person narration.

But perhaps also, OK seems suited to the end of the world, at least in McCarthy's vision, as it fades from gray to black.

THE PRACTICAL OK

DURING THE TWENTIETH CENTURY, OK MADE ITSELF EVER more useful by keeping pace with new technology and an old sport. OK is at home in radio, baseball, outer space, and above all the computer. These places have made OK all the more OK, less and less with any aura of slang, and of course unfathomably distant from its joking birth.

Early in the twentieth century, radio became commercial and took OK with it, in the form of the OK sign. In the heyday of live radio broadcasting in 1946, Paul Beath described the context in the journal *American Speech*:

Anyone who has witnessed a radio broadcast of any complexity knows that the director sits behind a sound proof glass with the engineer and directs his artists—vocal and instrumental—by means of a sign language. . . .

[O]nce the director has regulated the tempo, volume, or tone of his production to his liking, he tells his artists by means of a sign that the show is going "O.K." This he does by joining his thumb and forefinger in the shape of an "O" with other fingers extended.

This happens also to be the sign for OK in American Sign Language. And it's also the basis for a pitch in baseball known as the "OK change." A change, or change-up, is a pitch thrown like a fastball but slower, the change of pace intended to disrupt the batter's timing. What makes the pitch slower is the grip. A fastball uses the index and middle fingers, along with the thumb. A change, on the other hand, uses the middle and ring fingers, keeping the stronger index finger out of the action. In an OK change, also known as a circle change, the pitcher touches index finger and thumb at the side of the ball, thus making the OK sign and giving that pitch its name.

When Americans began traveling in space, they brought OK with them. In fact, thanks to the manned space program of the 1960s, OK gave birth to its most assertive offspring yet, AOK.

The introduction of AOK was something of an accident. On May 5, 1961, astronaut Alan Shepard made the first American flight into space. It was a suborbital flight, to be sure, lasting all of fifteen minutes and reaching an altitude of only 116 miles, but it was a perfect flight and a national triumph. And it was broadcast on live television.

Shepard himself didn't use AOK. In his communications with mission control, Shepard first used *go*: "Fuel is go. Oxygen is go.

All systems are go." Then he switched to plain OK: "Pitch is OK. Yaw is OK. Roll is OK." And later, just "OK, OK, OK." "Oxygen is still OK." Finally, it was *good*: "Main chute is good."

Meanwhile, however, back on earth, a spokesman for the National Aeronautics and Space Agency introduced AOK to the public. Apparently the engineering staff at NASA had been prefixing OK with A to make sure it would be understood amid radio static. NASA public affairs officer John "Shorty" Powers told reporters that Shepard had said everything was AOK, and the term immediately caught on. As Tom Wolfe wrote in *The Right Stuff*, "'A-Okay' became shorthand for Shepard's triumph over the odds and for astronaut coolness under stress."

And as befits its ubiquity, OK was present in the first human conversation on the moon. Indeed, it was the very first word spoken after the lunar module landed on July 20, 1969. Eric Jones's careful transcription of the conversation between Neil Armstrong and Buzz Aldrin in the lunar module, landing on the moon, and with Charles Duke, the voice of mission control back on Earth, goes as follows:

> *Aldrin:* Contact light. [A probe beneath the lunar module makes contact with the surface.]
> *Armstrong:* Shutdown. [And with engines off, the module settles down.]
> *Aldrin:* OK. Engine stop.

The astronauts continue with technical details:

> *Aldrin:* ACA out of detent.
> *Armstrong:* Out of detent. Auto.
> *Aldrin:* Mode control, both auto. Descent engine command override, off. Engine arm, off. 413 is in.
> *Duke:* We copy you down, Eagle.

Armstrong: Engine arm is off. Houston, Tranquility Base here. The Eagle has landed.

Duke: Roger, Twan . . . Tranquility. We copy you on the ground. You got a bunch of guys about to turn blue. We're breathing again. Thanks a lot.

Aldrin: Thank you.

Duke: You're looking good here.

And the conversation resumes with more OKs:

Armstrong: OK. (To Aldrin) Let's get on with it. (To Houston) OK. We're going to be busy for a minute.

And then, toward the end of the twentieth century, came the personal computer, with OK hitching a ride. Nowadays any computer or cell phone, and practically any device connected to the Internet, will offer choices with the "OK button." It seems natural now, but that wasn't the first thought of the software engineers who pioneered interactive computing.

It was the early 1980s and Apple's engineers were developing the first personal computer with a graphical user interface, the Lisa, using the now nearly universal mouse-guided system. With the new point-and-click technique, the question arose: when you click, what do you point at?

According to the story recounted by Andy Hertzfeld, a member of the Lisa applications team, it was manager Larry Tesler who insisted on testing the software with real users. The feedback from that testing resulted in the OK button.

The developers first offered users a choice between "Do It" and "Cancel." But when they tested those options, they discovered that "Do It" puzzled some users. One complained, "Why is the computer calling me a dolt?" The problem was solved when OK took the place of "Do It."

Hertzfeld says that the developers had avoided OK "because we thought it was too colloquial." But OK has many advantages. It is short, easy to recognize with its unique and distinctive combination of *O* and *K*, universally understood, and perfectly suited to a situation where you might be more or less enthusiastic but still want to do it. No wonder it caught on. And though nowadays you will sometimes click "Select" or "Approve" or "Agree" or "Enter," OK remains the most likely to appear in a dialogue box.

Bill DeRouchey, on his website Push. Click. Touch, offers this paean to the OK button:

> All interaction with technology is a conversation. You ask a device to do something. It responds with a question or some choices. In most situations, your simplest response is to simply say OK. The OK button is the handshake. You and the device have worked together to a mutual agreement. "Do you want to save this phone number?" OK. "Do you want to print your document two-sided?" OK.
>
> It's the one button that requires nearly no translation. Luckily, it's also one of the most compact words available. OK. Two letters that will fit on any button. OK is not just a word anymore. It's an icon. A wordicon. . . .
>
> Select and Enter are commands to machines. OK is a conversation with your friend, technology.
>
> OK? OK.

In a follow-up comment, DeRouchey adds:

> OK is acquiescing to the machine, forming a partnership. . . . It changed the relationship between person and computer, away from the master and slave mentality toward a friendlier world where the computer is a partner.
>
> I'm not sure we're there yet.

THE WORLD—
AND ENGLAND

NOWADAYS OK HAS SPREAD TO NUMEROUS LANGUAGES THROUGH-
out the world. From pole to pole, from the precincts of Paris to the
homes of Hong Kong, from the plains of Serengeti to the steppes
of Siberia, from the tip of Tierra del Fuego to the top of Mount
Everest, wherever humans discourse in whatever language, it may
well be punctuated with OK.

Speakers of Dutch, German, Swedish, Polish, Finnish, Italian,
Spanish, Welsh, Hebrew, Korean, and Japanese, among many others,
say OK, with pronunciations adapted to their languages. Hebrew is a
typical example. From Ashley Crandall's blog about her trip to Israel:

> The most important thing that came out of that trip is we
> figured out how to say "okay" in Hebrew. . . . In Hebrew it

would go something like chet, o vowel, kaf, yud with this
other vowel that when combined make an "a" sound. Make
sure the sound of the chhhh comes from the back of your
mouth and is obnoxiously overdone. People that speak German and Scandinavian do very well with this sound. Spanish
speakers come very close to the right sound as long as their
English isn't too good and they still mispronounce words that
start with an "h" like hotdog . . . try chhhotdog.

In Hebrew, as in many other languages, OK coexists with
native terminology. As Ari Kernerman of Kernerman Publishing
in Tel Aviv explains:

> The Hebrew word that OK has replaced is *b'seder*. *Seder* is
> "order," and *b'seder* is "in order." So *b'seder* could be translated
> as "alright." But OK is now more common than *b'seder*.

To Americans, OK is OK. Although it is central to our way of
life, to us it conjures up nothing special, because it is so natural, so
much a part of our daily dealings. Despite its odd and obtrusive
spelling, we take it for granted.

Not always the rest of the world. From the nineteenth century to the present day, as an export to other countries and languages, OK has carried with it a distinctively American aura. It
has embodied something special—sometimes American simplicity, pragmatism, and optimism, and at other times a certain
glamour.

That must have been in the minds of a young couple from
Holland who rated the Hotel Charles in Budapest as a "very
okay 3 star hotel!" Or the editors of a Russian humor and satire
magazine, published in the United States, who decided to call
it *Okay!* Or for that matter, the editors of a British celebrity

weekly named *OK!* that has recently had success with an American edition.

OK! had an awkward launch in America in 2005, partly because Americans were puzzled by the title. Its American rivals are named *People, Us Weekly, Star, National Enquirer, In Touch*—nothing even remotely resembling OK. Interviewed in 2007 for the *Sunday Times* of London, New York editor Sarah Ivens said that American advertisers didn't understand the title. And why should they? As we have seen, OK hasn't done much to sell a product. It wasn't the title but the revamping of the magazine to feature American celebrities that has made *OK!* a success.

The rest of the world had no such trouble with the title. *OK!* magazine has helped spread OK around the world, with editions in twenty countries and a weekly total circulation of some thirty million.

But then the British have always been a bit batty about OK. For them, at least at first, OK was a swell import—quite literally swell. It was popularized as a "swell" expression in England around 1870 in a music hall song by Alfred Vance, "The Great Vance." He and other music hall performers of the day, known as "Lions Comique," took on the air and appearance of a London "swell," a dandy dressed in the latest fashions and imagining himself to be a ladies' man. In the final chorus of his famous song, "Walking in the Zoo," Vance assures the audience he is "as great a swell as ever." His performances of this song apparently deserve credit for popularizing not only OK but also the abbreviation "Zoo" for "Zoological Society's Gardens." The song also uses the newly introduced Americanism *skedaddle*.

In the sheet music for "Walking in the Zoo," OK appears with commas rather than periods after each of the letters, apparently because its use was so unfamiliar to the author, Hugh Willoughby Sweny, and the publisher.

Cover of Sheet Music for "Walking in the Zoo," 1871

1. The Stilton, sir, the cheese, the O, K, thing to do,
On Sunday afternoon, is to toddle in the Zoo,
Weekdays may do for "Cads," but not for me and you,
So dress'd right down the road, we show them who is who.

Chorus.

The Walking in the Zoo, Walking in the Zoo,
The O, K, thing on Sunday is the walking in the Zoo,
Walking in the Zoo, Walking in the Zoo,
The O, K, thing on Sunday is the walking in the Zoo.

2. So when there came to Town, my pretty cousin Loo
I took her off to spend a Sunday at the Zoo,
I show'd her the aquarium, the Tiger, the Zebu,
The Eliphant [*sic*], the Eland, that cuss the Kangaroo.

Chorus.

That Sunday in the Zoo, That Sunday in the Zoo,
It's jolly with a pretty girl walking in the Zoo
Walking in the Zoo, Walking in the Zoo,
The O, K, thing on Sunday is the walking in the Zoo.

3. I show'd her the swell-es-ses, and all the fashions new
Girls with golden tresses, girls with black hair too.
Walnut gives the black, Champagne the golden hue
All the beautiful forever that Madame Rachel knew.

Chorus.

Oh! The Walking in the Zoo, Walking in the Zoo,
The monkeys put us to the blush on Sunday at the Zoo.
Walking in the Zoo, Walking in the Zoo,
The O, K, thing on Sunday is the walking in the Zoo.

4. So in the monkey house our going in to woo,
Piling up the agony, swearing to be true,

Agony indeed! for the cheerful Cockatoo.

Rudely caught my ear a nip and bit it through and
through.

Chorus.

Oh! that cheerful Cockatoo, That awful Cockatoo

The horror and the agony that Sunday at the Zoo.

Walking in the Zoo, Walking in the Zoo,

The O, K, thing on Sunday is the walking in the Zoo.

5. My cousin bolted off without any more ado,

And I skedaddled also looking very blue,

So sympathizing friends I bid you all adieu.

Don't mention this occurrence if you meet me at the Zoo,

Chorus.

If you meet me at the Zoo, You meet me at the Zoo,

I'm as great a swell as ever on Sunday at the Zoo.

Walking in the Zoo, Walking in the Zoo,

The O, K, thing on Sunday is the walking in the Zoo.

(The zoological gardens in Regent's Park were open to the public on weekdays, but only members of the Zoological Society
could enter on Sunday, hence the swell superiority of that day.
Stilton is of course a famous blue cheese. Madame Rachel was
famous for her prominently advertised book *Beautiful for Ever*,
"on Female Grace and Beauty." She also sold many beauty products, such as a "Magnetic Rock Dew Water of Sahara, for removing Wrinkles.")

"Walking in the Zoo" has had a modest revival in the present
day. In 2004 a song "The OK Thing to Do on Sunday Afternoon
Is to Toddle in the Zoo" was released in an album of that name by
the duo known as My Little Airport, described as a "Hong Kong–
based indie pop band." To be sure, the Chinese words of the song

make only a glancing reference to the zoo in recalling a lost relationship:

> Your photo is kept with a love letter, each day I see it once again.
> The zoo we strolled 2 years ago, till now where did we go?
> I did wrote about you everyday in my diary, but to give up on you is a hopeless dream, Just like a dull solo. . . .

The Slang Dictionary, Etymological, Historical, and Anecdotal, published in London in 1874, about the same time as "Walking in the Zoo," reflects this positive British view of OK as well as the standard story about President Jackson (or at least "an official") marking OK on documents:

> O. K., a matter to be o. k. (OLL KORRECT, *i.e.*, all correct), must be on the "square," and perfectly in order. This is an Americanism, and is derived from the initials o. k., said to have been marked on a document by an official to signify that all was right and proper.

Another British attitude toward OK is demonstrated in the movie *Gosford Park*. It's a twenty-first-century movie, released in 2001, but it presumes to depict life at an English country house in 1932. OK occurs two times in the script, which was written by an Englishman, Julian Fellowes. In one of the opening scenes, traveling to Gosford Park, Constance, Countess of Trentham, is frustrated in her attempt to have the top of her motorcar removed. An American movie producer who is also going to Gosford Park pulls up. Seeing her frustration, he asks: "Hello. Is everything all right? Are—are you OK?"

Apparently puzzled by the expression, Lady Trentham replies, "Am I what?"

So Lady Trentham's lady's maid, Mary Maceachran, translates: "We're all right, thank you."

The implication is that OK is either unknown to Lady Trentham or, more likely, an Americanism not suitable for cultivated speech. Still, it is clear that Mary has no trouble understanding it, and OK comes up later when she is talking with another servant about Sir William McCordle and his wife, Lady Sylvia, who preside over Gosford Park. Mary asks, "What's she like to work for?" and Elsie, the head housemaid at Gosford Park, replies, "She's horrible. But he's—he's OK."

One of the oddest uses for OK in the UK emerged apparently in the 1930s, apparently in Glasgow. Urbandictionary.com explains it this way:

> The phrase's first recorded use was in 1975, but it is rumored to have originated as early as the 1930's among the Glasgow "Razor Gangs." Rival gangs were known to tag each other's turf with "(gang name) Rules, Ok?" during disputes over territory as a part of gang warfare.

Examples offered by Urbandictionary.com are *Dandys Rule, OK?* and *KC RULES OK*. "Brian from Shawnee" posted on the Phrase Finder website in 2004:

> My suggestion is from UK urban gang "turf" rivalries and flick knife wars of the 1950s where the practice was to mark your gang's territory with slogans painted on buildings with phrases like: "Red Blades rule OK?" Serious stuff in those days.

Whatever the origin—the earliest published evidence is from the 1970s—nowadays *rules OK* continues to be used in Britain, and it has gone proper, often with tongue in cheek. The *Oxford English Dictionary* quotes the *Sunday Express* from 1976: "And when he left the train . . . he gave . . . a look which said . . 'First Class Rules—O.K.?'" And *The Times* from 1981: "It is a case of the tobacco industry rules, OK."

The Stray Cats, an American rockabilly band, wrote the song "Rockabilly Rules OK" after they moved to England in the 1980s. Here are some of the lyrics from their 1989 album *Blast Off*:

> We're naming this song rockabilly rules OK.
> Well rockabilly rules OK.
> Rockabilly's cool. Oh yeah.
> Rockabilly rocks. Let's bop.
> Well rockabilly billy bop. Let's bop.

There's a children's book, *Titus Rules OK*, published in 2002 and written by Dick King-Smith (an Englishman, of course—a former farmer from Gloucestershire). Titus is the Queen's dog, a corgi. He learns from his mother how to rule:

> "The Queen, you see, may be responsible for the welfare not just of her family but of all the citizens of the United Kingdom and her realms overseas. But, in her eyes, it is our welfare that is at the top of her priorities and most important to her. She is our servant."
>
> "Gosh!" said Titus. "D'you mean she'll do whatever we tell her to?"
>
> "Certainly," said his mother.
>
> "If I told her to do something, she'd do it, would she, Mum?"
>
> "If you told her in the right way."
>
> "How d'you mean?"
>
> "Politely. Her Majesty does not like being barked at or yapped at. You'll have noticed that just now, when she dished

out the biscuits, we all kept as quiet as mice. Any time you want a biscuit, just go and sit quite silently in front of the Queen and gaze up into her eyes with a pleading look."

At the end, Titus has become so much the Queen's favorite that he gets to sleep with her. And the Queen herself late at night spray-paints in gold on the wall of the courtyard, "Titus Rules OK."

One of the best-known uses of OK in the UK was by the Monty Python comedy troupe in their "Lumberjack Song," first presented on television in December 1969. A man reveals his day-dream of being a lumberjack in Canada with these words:

> I'm a lumberjack and I'm OK,
> I sleep all night and I work all day.
> I cut down trees, I eat my lunch,
> I go to the lavatory.
> On Wednesdays I go shopping
> And have buttered scones for tea.

He continues in this vein, as a girlfriend and a chorus of Canadian Mounties echo his words. "He's a lumberjack and he's OK," they declare, less and less enthusiastically as he describes his other activities, until they turn away in disgust:

> I put on women's clothing,
> And hang around in bars. . . .
> I cut down trees, I wear high heels,
> Suspendies and a bra.
> I wish I'd been a girlie,
> Just like my dear pappa.

One final British example is Oakie Doke, originally a cartoon series in stop-motion animation for the BBC in 1995–96.

If you have a problem and you need a helping hand,
Cross the dell and ring the bell—he'll understand.
Don't worry, 'cos here comes Mr. Doke,
The friendliest of folk is Mr. Oakie Doke.

And who exactly is Mr. Oakie Doke? The website Toonhound explains:

Oakie Doke is a jolly helpful woodland chap—a wisp, a forest spirit or sprite—garbed in oak leaves with twig limbs, leafy ears and an acorn crowned head. Oakie dwells in a splendid hollowed oak tree house with a terrific helter-skelter built around the outside upon which rides every episode, down to meet his forest friends.

Okey-dokey? Well, that's not the end of it. As the next chapter will explain, OK found its way into a very British exposition of a way of life.

THE LIFEMANSHIP OK

CONSIDERING THE PECULIAR USES TO WHICH THE ENGLISH HAVE put OK, it is perhaps not so surprising that a British wag was the first to hit upon a way to use OK in the service of expounding a way of life—a philosophy, if you will.

Throughout its history, OK has remained conspicuously absent from philosophy. Two letters born of a joke and used for practical purposes hardly make for a view of life or a way of life. Indeed, to this day serious philosophical discourse, like all formal discourse, generally avoids using OK at all. But OK plays a significant supporting role in the pseudo-serious practical philosophy known as Lifemanship.

Lifemanship was explained in a work of deadpan British humor: *Some Notes on Lifemanship*, a 1950 book by Stephen Potter.

This was a sequel to his 1947 *The Theory and Practice of Gamesmanship: Or, The Art of Winning Games Without Actually Cheating.* Gamesmanship was about winning in sports; Lifemanship extended that method to all of life.

Both books expound a strategy encapsulated in the title of his 1955 book *One-Upmanship: Being Some Account of the Activities and Teaching of the Lifemanship Correspondence College of One-upness and Gameslifemastery,* where he offers advice on "how to be one up—how to make the other man feel that something has gone wrong, however slightly."

One tactic for one-upping, Potter says in *Lifemanship*, is to use what he calls "O.K.-words" and "O.K.-names" in conversation:

NOTE ON O.K.-WORDS.

My use of the word "diathesis" reminds me that this is now on the O.K. list for conversationmen. We hope to publish, monthly, a list of words which may be brought up at any point in the conversation and used with effect because no one quite understands what they mean, albeit these words have been in use for a sufficiently long time, at any rate by Highbrowmen, say ten years, for our audience to have seen them once or twice and already felt uneasy about them. We are glad to suggest two words for November: *Mystique, Classique.*

In a later chapter on Writership, instructing a literary critic how to "be on top of, or better than, the person criticised," Potter declares, "The absolute O.K.-ness of French literature, particularly modern French, and indeed of France generally, cannot be too much emphasized." And he adds, "Just as there are O.K.-words in conversationship, so there are O.K.-*people* to mention in Newstatesmanship. Easily the most O.K. for 1945–50 are Rilke and Kafka. It is believed that they will still be absolutely O.K. for another five years, in fact it is doubtful if there have been any more O.K.-names in recent times." In a footnote he lists

> types of authors who are not O.K.-names whom it is O.K. to pitch into. It is all right to pitch into:
>
> Any author who has written a book about dogs.
>
> Any author who has written a book on natural history, illustrated with woodcuts.
>
> Any author who has written a life of Napoleon, Byron, or Dr. Johnson, without footnotes or bibliography.
>
> Any author of a life of anybody not yet dead.
>
> Any author of a book on Sussex.
>
> Any author of a book of unrhymed and irregular verse in the style of 1923.
>
> Any author of a book of thoughtful open-air poems in the style of 1916.

Every sentence of his books is written with tongue in cheek. His use of OK in a pseudo-philosophical treatise only adds to its irony. And yet it is possible to see a common thread, accidental or otherwise, leading to the next and completely serious use of OK as a view of the world.

THE PSYCHOLOGICAL
OK

LIFEMANSHIP **WAS A SATIRICAL BOOK ABOUT PLAYING THE GAME OF** life. The psychiatrist Eric Berne, however, took the idea of games seriously, inadvertently starting a process that has led to what could be called the American philosophy of the twenty-first century. It helped transform Americans from xenophobes to xenophiles.

The story of the mind-altering development of OK begins like this: In the 1950s Dr. Eric Berne, a psychiatrist living in the trendy artistic community of Carmel, California, led a revolution in psychology, or at least a minor uprising. Instead of concentrating on therapy for the individual, he diverted attention to interactions between individuals. He called his innovation transactional analysis.

For several years after the 1958 publication of his paper on the new approach and the 1961 publication of his book *Transactional*

Analysis in Psychotherapy, TA was little known beyond the community of his professional colleagues. But it became a public sensation in 1964 with the book *Games People Play*. The subtitle modestly declared its scope: *The Psychology of Human Relationships*.

That plain, clear, and yet enticing title is one reason why the book soon became a national best seller. The other was that it was just as plain and clear on the inside. Freud had postulated the id, the ego, and the superego. Jung delved into analytical psychology, archetypes, animus, and anima. But you didn't have to be an expert to understand Berne's simpler explanation of states of mind and how they predispose people to play games with each other.

Berne says that everyone's personality contains three "ego states," named simply Parent, Adult, and Child. The Parent implanted itself in our minds from what our parents said or did while we were growing up. In the Parent mode, we ourselves act as parents, issuing instructions, criticisms, and occasionally compliments as we remember our parents (or parental substitutes) doing during our childhood.

The Child is the way we remember our own feelings in response to what our parents said or did while we were growing up. In the Child mode, we act like children, frequently feeling helpless, guilty, and inadequate.

In contrast with both the Parent and the Child, who act based on subjective memories from the past, is the Adult. The Adult is the grown-up, making decisions based not on childhood feelings but on objective analysis of the current situation.

At any particular moment, as we interact with others, we are in one of those three states. When we are in the Parent mode, we feel superior to others and tell them what to do. When we are in the Child mode, we feel inadequate and helpless, or sometimes playful. And when people interact Parent to Child, Parent to Parent, or Child to Child, instead of Adult to Adult, there are problems. In the Parent or Child modes, people play games that can repeat themselves endlessly without a satisfactory resolution.

Take the game Berne called "Why Don't You—Yes But," whose dynamic is clear from the title. It is played by one or more people taking the Parental role, offering advice on a particular problem, and one person taking the role of a helpless Child, coming up with reasons for being unable to accept any of the advice. From the Child's point of view, the goal of the game is not to solve the problem—that would happen Adult to Adult—but to comfortably confirm that the problem will persist and the Child can continue to complain about it.

Or there is "If It Weren't for You," played between husband and wife. One spouse, let's say the husband, is domineering and prohibits the other from going out or taking risks. The wife complains but is secretly gratified; she has chosen a domineering spouse in order to be prevented from doing things she fears, while having the opportunity to complain. The domineering spouse plays the Parent and the subordinate spouse the Child. Secretly, though, the domineering spouse is a Child too, afraid of being deserted. So says Dr. Berne.

Such games get us nowhere and are doomed to endless repetition, Berne says. So he provides antidotes, bringing in the Adult to break up the game. In "Why Don't You—Yes But," for example, the people giving advice can break out of the closed loop by saying, "That is a difficult problem. What are you going to do about it?" In "If It Weren't for You," the domineering spouse can end the game simply by saying, "Go ahead and do it."

Berne explains that the Adult within us allows us to look at situations not as prisoners of the past, governed by childish anxieties and parental strictures, but as free agents, free to interact in a healthy way in the present. Through Transactional Analysis, people can learn to recognize the unhealthy games they play with family and friends and learn to escape them. But then, of course, the participants are no longer in the comfort of a familiar game. And Berne is pessimistic: he worries that most people are too comfortable with their games to want to change.

"Why Don't You—Yes But" and "If It Weren't for You" are the first two games Berne studied. His book includes a hundred games, with similar self-explanatory titles. Most are destructive, played Child to Parent, Child to Child, or Parent to Parent. There are Life Games like "Alcoholic," "Now I've Got You, You Son of a Bitch," and "See What You Made Me Do." There are Marital Games like "If It Weren't for You," "Look How Hard I've Tried," and (said ironically) "Sweetheart." Party Games include "Ain't It Awful" and "Schlemiel." Sexual Games include "Let's You and Him Fight." As for Consulting Room Games, Berne draws on his professional experience to describe "I'm Only Trying to Help You," "Stupid," and five more.

All these are patterns of interaction performed by people who are usually unaware they are playing these games. Transactional Analysis aims to bring these patterns to the attention of the players so that they can end harmful games and replace them with good games like "Happy to Help," "Homely Sage," and "They'll Be Glad They Knew Me."

Nearly half a century after its publication, the insights of *Games People Play* remain pertinent and persuasive today, and their presentation remains engaging. No wonder the book has sold more than five million copies since its initial press run of just three thousand.

OK. So what does any of this have to do with OK? Nothing, so far. OK (spelled in its less conspicuous form *okay*) makes just two very minor appearances in *Games People Play*. Once it is part of one line in an eight-line greeting ritual: "'Well, take cara yourself.' (Okay.)" The other time it is in a bit of dialogue illustrating an antidote to the game "Schlemiel": "It's okay, tonight you can embarrass my wife, ruin the furniture and wreck the rug, but please don't say 'I'm sorry.'" Neither of these trivial uses of OK would make Berne's book a candidate for mention here. But it is important because it led to another, even more popular book on transactional analysis, one that chose OK as its focus and in so doing, gave new meaning and influence to OK.

I'm OK, You're OK

The book, by Thomas A. Harris, was titled even more simply than Berne's: *I'm OK, You're OK*. And it was much bolder. In *I'm OK, You're OK* Harris aimed to change the world for the better—and chose OK as the instrument of change.

It was an inspired choice, and a memorable one. In the entire history of OK, it is the only use of OK worthy to be included in a collection of famous quotations. The title has in fact eclipsed the book to take on a life of its own.

I'm OK, You're OK has sold even more copies than *Games People Play*—at least seven million, by a conservative estimate. Nevertheless, not too many people nowadays know the details of transactional analysis presented in *I'm OK, You're OK*. But on its own, the simple idea that title expresses has made OK a powerful voice for multiculturalism and diversity. Indeed, it could be argued that with *I'm OK, You're OK* as a catalyst, in the twenty-first century OK became a whole two-letter American philosophy of tolerance, even admiration, for difference.

Harris writes with the assurance of one who rests his conclusions on scientific evidence. Electronic probes of the brain, he reports, have demonstrated "that the brain functions as a high-fidelity recorder, putting on tape, as it were, every experience from the time of birth, possibly even before birth." It is these memories of our earliest years, he assures us, that put in our heads the submissive Child, the dominant Parent, and the rational Adult. Like Berne, Harris explains that we employ one or another of these when we interact with others.

And then Harris goes further, to assert that people often assume an emotional stance not just in individual transactions but throughout life, based on those mental tape recordings from childhood. Here is where he introduces OK:

> Transactional Analysis constructs the following classification of the four possible life positions held with respect to oneself and others:
>
> 1. I'M NOT OK—YOU'RE OK
> 2. I'M NOT OK—YOU'RE NOT OK
> 3. I'M OK—YOU'RE NOT OK
> 4. I'M OK—YOU'RE OK
>
> . . .
>
> I believe that by the end of the second year of life, or sometime during the third year, the child has decided on one of the first three positions. . . . It stays with him the rest of his life, unless he later consciously changes it to the fourth position. People do not shift back and forth.

As Berne's book demonstrates, Transactional Analysis has no need to be expressed in terms of OK. But it was Harris's brilliant idea to reduce the different attitudes toward life to the simplest elements, OK or not OK. With that inspiration, Harris added a new meaning to OK, one that took it from being merely utilitarian to a way of looking at life and the world.

Harris could have used some other expression to characterize his four life positions. In so doing, he would have followed the example of earlier architects of assertiveness and avoided OK because of its potential weakness. Harris could have chosen "I'm good—you're good" or I'm wonderful—you're wonderful," to mention just two of many possibilities. He could have harnessed the power of "positive thinking" with affirmations like "Every day, in every way, I am getting better and better" or, for that matter, Al Franken's parody on *Saturday Night Live*, in the character of Stuart Smalley: "I'm good enough, I'm smart enough, and doggone it, people like me!"

The vocabulary for positive thinking goes on and on. To take a few examples from the website Success Consciousness:

My body is healthy and functioning in a very good way.

I radiate love and happiness.

I have a wonderful and satisfying job.

Wealth is pouring into my life.

The problem with such affirmations is that they can be too positive for their own good. They are likely to inspire doubt rather than assurance in people not convinced of the power of positive thinking. But OK, while clearly affirmative, avoids this difficulty. It is neutral concerning the degree of affirmation. The OK position therefore allows for a great variety of mental states, encompassing feeling great as well barely getting along. (Smalley, for example, uses OK to keep his spirits up: "Okay . . . for those of you who watch the show regularly, you know that I don't have guests. I always do the show alone . . . and that's . . . o-kay.")

So by using the value-free OK, Harris can be convincing when he assures the reader that it's possible to reach the desired fourth state, "I'm OK—you're OK." There's a lot of room for imperfection in OK while still being on the right side.

Perhaps it is the low threshold of OK that makes Harris optimistic that it can change the world. Here is how he does it, in a chapter on moral values:

> **The Adult's approach to the worth of persons . . . would follow these lines.**
>
> **I am a person. You are a person. Without you I am not a person, for only through you is language made possible and only through language is thought made possible, and only through thought is humanness made possible. You have made me important. Therefore, I am important and you are important. If I devalue you, I devalue myself. This is the rationale of the position I'M OK—YOU'RE OK.**

Thanks to the flexible assertiveness of OK, Harris is able to stretch OK to make "I'm OK—you're OK" the equivalent of "I'm important—you're important."

A little later he declares, "The American myth seems to me to be grounded in the WE'RE OK—YOU'RE NOT OK position." He argues instead, "If we see that I'M OK—YOU'RE OK is at last within the realm of possibility, do we dare look for change, something new under the sun, something to stop the violence threatening to destroy what has taken millions of years to build? . . . We believe we have found an opening." And so he had, thanks to the flexibility and ambiguity of the term he chose as his focus—OK.

Berne, in contrast, was a pessimist. He doubted that most people would give up the comfort of games for the better life of awareness, spontaneity, and intimacy, and concludes *Games People Play* with the declaration "This may mean that there is no hope for the human race, but there is hope for individual members of it."

Harris took the opposite view, to say the least. He proclaims in his preface:

> If the relationship between two people can be made creative, fulfilling, and free of fear, then it follows that this can work for two relationships, or three or one hundred or, we are convinced, for relationships that affect entire social groups, even nations. The problems of the world—and they are chronicled daily in headlines of violence and despair—essentially are the problems of individuals. If individuals can change, the course of the world can change. This is a hope worth sustaining.

Nearly half a century later, the world hasn't changed quite as Harris envisioned. Neither the whole world nor the whole country has gone en masse for transactional analysis therapy. But it turns out that therapy wasn't necessary to effect a change in attitudes. At the start of the 1960s in the United States, law and custom were quite different from what they are today. Discrimination against minorities and women was not only widely practiced but widely accepted. Today acceptance and indeed affirmation of differences have become pervasive, in law as well as in practice, and those values persist despite the encouragement to xenophobia caused by the threat of terrorism.

To say that "I'm OK—you're OK" is the cause of the change would not be OK. But to say that it has taken hold as a kind of mantra that everyone knows, even to parody it, would be OK indeed. It's a little harder to hold on to prejudice when you know it means taking the attitude "I'm OK—you're not OK."

Popular psychologies, like popular diets, come and go. Trans-actional analysis is alive and well but not nearly as well known to the general public as it was forty-odd years ago. Unless we've stud-ied or taken part in TA, we don't remember its complexities. But the simplicity of Harris's title lives on; we remember the simple message "I'm OK—you're OK."

And so in the twenty-first century we find ourselves in a world that is, or ought to be, OK. "I'm OK—you're OK" has led to the corollary "It's OK to . . ." We, and our children, can read books like Todd Parr's *It's Okay to Be Different* (2001) and its sequel, *The Okay Book* (2004), where we learn that it's OK, among other things, to be missing a tooth, to need a seeing-eye dog, to be adopted, and to have big ears (like a bunny).

Actually, to listen to various authorities, sometimes it's OK to be . . . whatever: "It's OK to be a tightwad for the holidays," the *Los Angeles Times* assured readers in 2008.

J. Jill advertised in May 2009: "Now through Sunday, May 17th: It's okay to wear white! Take $10 off our summer white denim."

An image consultant tells boomers, "It's OK to go gray" (gray-haired).

Marie Osmond tells *People*, "It's OK to be alone."

Nutritionists say, "It's OK to go a little wild about nuts."

The author of *Fixing Your Feet* says "It's OK to go barefoot; in fact, it is fun and refreshing and makes your feet happy."

The Lifehacker website has a lesson for Small Business 101: "It's OK to be clueless."

And Frank Bruno declares in a book published in 2004, "It's OK to be neurotic."

This is the self-empowering OK, a mantra of tolerance and acceptance unprecedented in our history. Unlike existentialism, phenomenology, humanism, pragmatism, and other isms, OK-ism (as we may term it) has developed without any assistance from philosophers, without any discussion among the literati or cognoscenti, without even an entry in Wikipedia. But it exerts a strong influence on us and our twenty-first-century world. OK has made tolerance more tolerable.

Nowadays a whole campaign can be built around this positive sense of OK:

> P.E.O. Record readers may recall the eye-catching banners and call-outs appearing in 2005 that proclaimed simply "It's OK." These messages were developed to serve as teasers for what was to come.
>
> Upon arrival in Vancouver, delegates and guests at the 2005 Convention of International chapter of the P.E.O. Sisterhood encountered more "It's OK" announcements. From hotel room key holders to signs and placards, the message "It's OK" appeared everywhere! Later the rest of the message was revealed: "It's OK to Talk About P.E.O." . . .
>
> Because the "It's OK to Talk About P.E.O." message and campaign was so enthusiastically embraced by our membership, in 2007, a sequel communiqué was unveiled: "OK . . . LET'S GROW!" (*P.E.O. Record*, Sept.-Oct. 2009)

Of course, not everyone is happy with every new OK. Columnist Ellen Goodman protests the movie *Juno*'s acceptance of teen pregnancy:

> Whatever the cost to actual teenage mothers, it isn't paid by their stars. The only one paying a price for [Jamie Lynn] Spears's pregnancy is OK! magazine, which reportedly put up $1 million for her pronouncement. (I'm OK! You're OK! Even if you're 16 and pregnant.)

THE AMERICAN
PHILOSOPHY

*Je pense qu'il n'y a pas, dans le monde civilisé, de pays où l'on
s'occupe moins de philosophie qu'aux États-Unis.* [I think that there
is no country in the civilized world where less attention is paid
to philosophy than in the United States.]

—Alexis de Tocqueville, *De la démocratie en Amérique,* Tome II (1840)

TO THIS DAY, ALEXIS DE TOCQUEVILLE'S OBSERVATION REMAINS
true. Except in a few obscure corners of academia, Americans still
do not trouble themselves about philosophy. But without stopping to philosophize, Americans were busy then, as now, exemplifying a philosophy of pragmatism. And that philosophy found its
perfect expression in the two letters OK, coincidentally created
almost at the same time Tocqueville's treatise on democracy in
America was published.

Consider this: OK is practical, not sentimental. It means that
something works. It doesn't imply or demand perfection, nor does
it imply disappointment. It's just . . . perfectly OK.

Even its form is just right: one word consisting of a mere two
letters, almost as short as an expression can be. Best of all, it

exemplifies imperfection successfully overcome, blatant misspelling not holding it back from becoming America's most successful invention.

And that's just the half of it. Thanks to the accident of the now-faded fad for transactional analysis, "I'm OK—you're OK" has become the American philosophy of the new century. We really believe that "I'm OK—you're OK" is the best way to treat ourselves and others. We want ourselves to be OK. We are concerned with building self-esteem and are concerned when someone doesn't have it. Religion sometimes calls us sinners, even miserable sinners—but we have learned to get over it. I'm OK, thank you!

And as for you, you're OK too. Not just OK, you're AOK. Even, or especially, if you're different from me.

Nowadays not only do we allow others to be different, we celebrate diversity. We have laws that require us to respect differences, and we have admonitions to rejoice in them. And we teach "I'm OK, you're OK" to our children, for example in Todd Parr's first *Okay Book* (1999): it's OK to be short, it's OK to wear what you want, it's OK to come from a different place, it's OK to be a different color. OK is not merely toleration but celebration.

In an arena quite different from psychology, a whole course can be built around the "I'm OK—you're OK" theme. The World History Association, in partnership with the Woodrow Wilson Leadership Program for Teachers, features on its website an interdisciplinary course in world history and literature for high school students with the title "I'm Okay, You're Okay: Teaching Tolerance Through World Religions." The teachers of the course, Pat Carney and Anne Wallin, explain:

> **Religion is an important aspect of historical and literary studies. No universal agreement exists about religion. To**

encourage norms of acceptance and tolerance in classroom discussions, we examine the vocabulary of intolerance, such as ethnocentrism and xenophobia. We study various belief systems to learn about these and to understand others. Our purpose is not to proselytize. We recognize that there are many views.

Perhaps thinking along these lines, a majority of Americans in 2008 decided it was OK to elect a president with a black father from Kenya and a white mother from Kansas.

So today we have two influential OKs: OK the embodiment of down-to-earth pragmatism and OK the voice of tolerance. Not bad for just two letters.

Forget the other American inventions: telegraph, telephone, typewriter, television, computer, smart phone, not to mention electric lighting, the hula hoop, variable-speed windshield wiper, and trick-or-treat. These merely influenced our lives; OK influences our thinking. It could be argued that OK is America's greatest invention.

I confess to a fondness for OK—so mighty yet so humble. Unconventional, but mild-mannered. Too humble even to show itself in grand speeches and declarations. We ought to celebrate OK Day every year on its birthday, March 23.

INDEX
....